UNCLE EARL

A Play in Two Acts
Suggested by the life and words of
Governor Earl K. Long of Louisiana

by
GEORGE SANCHEZ

Dramatic Publishing
Woodstock, Illinois • England • Australia • New Zealand
East Baton Rouge Parish Library
Baton Rouge, Louisiana

*** NOTICE ***

The amateur and stock acting rights to this work are controlled exclusively by THE DRAMATIC PUBLISHING COMPANY without whose permission in writing no performance of it may be given. Royalty must be paid every time a play is performed whether or not it is presented for profit and whether or not admission is charged. A play is performed any time it is acted before an audience. Current royalty rates, applications and restrictions may be found at our Web site: www.dramaticpublishing.com, or we may be contacted by mail at: DRAMATIC PUBLISHING COMPANY, P.O. Box 129, Woodstock IL 60098.

COPYRIGHT LAW GIVES THE AUTHOR OR THE AUTHOR'S AGENT THE EXCLUSIVE RIGHT TO MAKE COPIES. This law provides authors with a fair return for their creative efforts. Authors earn their living from the royalties they receive from book sales and from the performance of their work. Conscientious observance of copyright law is not only ethical, it encourages authors to continue their creative work. This work is fully protected by copyright. No alterations, deletions or substitutions may be made in the work without the prior written consent of the publisher. No part of this work may be reproduced or transmitted in any form or by any means, electronic or mechanical, including photocopy, recording, videotape, film, or any information storage and retrieval system, without permission in writing from the publisher. It may not be performed either by professionals or amateurs without payment of royalty. All rights, including, but not limited to, the professional, motion picture, radio, television, videotape, foreign language, tabloid, recitation, lecturing, publication and reading, are reserved.

For performance of any songs, music and recordings mentioned in this play which are in copyright, the permission of the copyright owners must be obtained or other songs and recordings in the public domain substituted.

©MMV by
GEORGE J. SANCHEZ
Printed in the United States of America
All Rights Reserved
(UNCLE EARL)

ISBN: 1-58342-288-9

IMPORTANT BILLING AND CREDIT REQUIREMENTS

All producers of the play *must* give credit to the Author of the play in all programs distributed in connection with performances of the play and in all instances in which the title of the play appears for purposes of advertising, publicizing or otherwise exploiting the play and/or a production. The name of the Author *must* also appear on a separate line, on which no other name appears, immediately following the title, and *must* appear in size of type not less than fifty percent the size of the title type. Biographical information on the Author, if included in the playbook, may be used in all programs. *In all programs this notice must appear:*

Produced by special arrangement with
THE DRAMATIC PUBLISHING COMPANY of Woodstock, Illinois

UNCLE EARL was first produced by the Slidell Little Theatre, Slidell, La., with the following cast, in order of appearance:

UNCLE EARL	Jack Cerny
AUNTIE ALICE	Lynne M. Lee
MIZ BLANCHE, Earl's wife	Kit McLellan
JOE ARTHUR, Earl's aide	P. Shawn McCrea
"TIMES-PICAYUNE"	Myron Miller
BOY	Jack Sconza
"CRAWDADDY," a state trooper	Allen Bryant
BILL, a friend of Earl	Belford Carver
BILL'S WIFE	Dana Peschke
ATTORNEY GENERAL	Fred Martinez
SADIE, a cook	Dana Peschke
FIRST PARTYGOER	Jeffrey P. Polito
SECOND PARTYGOER	Elizabeth Bigger
NURSE	Dana Peschke
ORDERLY	Jeffrey P. Polito
DOCTOR	Charles Vaught
PSYCHOLOGIST	Jeffrey P. Polito
LUCILLE, Earl's sister	Kim Mestier
HOSPITAL SUPERINTENDENT	Belford Carver
TOWNSPEOPLE	Elly Carroll, Elizabeth Bigger
SECOND REPORTER	Dana Peschke
HOTEL CLERK	Charles Vaught
OLD LADY	Kim Mestier
FANNY, an ecdysiast	Elly Carroll
BOOTY, her friend	Elizabeth Bigger
LITTLE EARL	Connor Macloud
BRUNO, Fanny's husband	Jeffrey P. Polito

The production was directed by the playwright and produced by Jack Cerny. Set design by Martin Cox and George Sanchez. Lighting design by George Sanchez. Music Consultant, Mel Rogers. Stage Manager, Kim Mestier. Production photographer, Paul Wood.

UNCLE EARL

CHARACTERS (in order of appearance)

Auntie ALICE: A handsome, middle-aged black woman, working for Earl's family; a surrogate mother to the young Earl

Uncle EARL: 60, governor of the state of Louisiana, a man who might be called distinguished with gray hair and a pleasant, open face, were he not rumpled and sweaty, with a certain air of desperation about him. At the time of the play, he had been governor three times and had a wide and devoted following

Miz BLANCHE: Earl's wife, an attractive middle-aged woman. She is no shrinking violet of a Southern belle. Very much her own person, hers is a forceful personality

JOE Arthur: 30s, Earl's aide, bespectacled, slouching, with a shambling grace to him, he is Earl's attorney and good right hand

"TIMES-PICAYUNE": 40s, a reporter of the old school, he is cynical, disheveled, fond of drink, and honest by his own lights

BOY: 12, of working-class origin, he is proud, energetic and not afraid to stand up for himself

"CRAWDADDY": 20s, a state trooper, corn-fed and open with an ingenuous air

The following roles were doubled in the original production:

BILL: 50s (younger in flashback), friend and political supporter of Earl's, he is a classic "pol" in appearance

ATTORNEY GENERAL: 50s, rotund and sweaty, yet dapper in his dress, he is very much dominated by Earl

LUCILLE: 60s, Earl's sister, still the schoolteacher she once was, open, loving and stern

DOCTOR: 40s, professional and trim, a near caricature of a medical man

PSYCHOLOGIST: 40s, professional, bearded, a near caricature of a "shrink"

FANNY: 20s, an ecdysiast, with an open, vulnerable quality that makes her more daughter than sex object

BOOTY: 20s, another stripper, vivacious, energetic, and none too bright

LITTLE EARL: 10-12, Earl as a boy in a Norman Rockwell-ish manner

BILL'S WIFE: 20s, attractive and dressed for a party in the 1920s style

PARTYGOERS: A man and woman in their 20s, attractive and dressed for a party in the 1950s style

SADIE: 40s, a rural, no-nonsense cook on Earl's "pea patch" farm

Hospital SUPERINTENDENT: 50s, a faceless bureaucrat

NURSE: 30s, professional, pert

ORDERLY: 30s, professional, husky

SECOND REPORTER: 30s, typical of the breed

PHOTOGRAPHER: 30s, typical of the breed

Hotel CLERK: 40s, faceless, typical of the breed

OLD LADY: 70s-80s, a feisty New Mexican

BRUNO: 40s, Fanny's husband, dressed in the sharp threads of a French Quarter character

TOWNSPEOPLE: various ages, local color

SETTING:
The mind of Uncle Earl, which encompasses the state of Louisiana and points West.

TIME:
Summer and fall, 1960, and time past.

ACT ONE: The Earl and his court.
ACT TWO: Magical mystery tour.

For Joe, Sylvie and Andy—who believed.

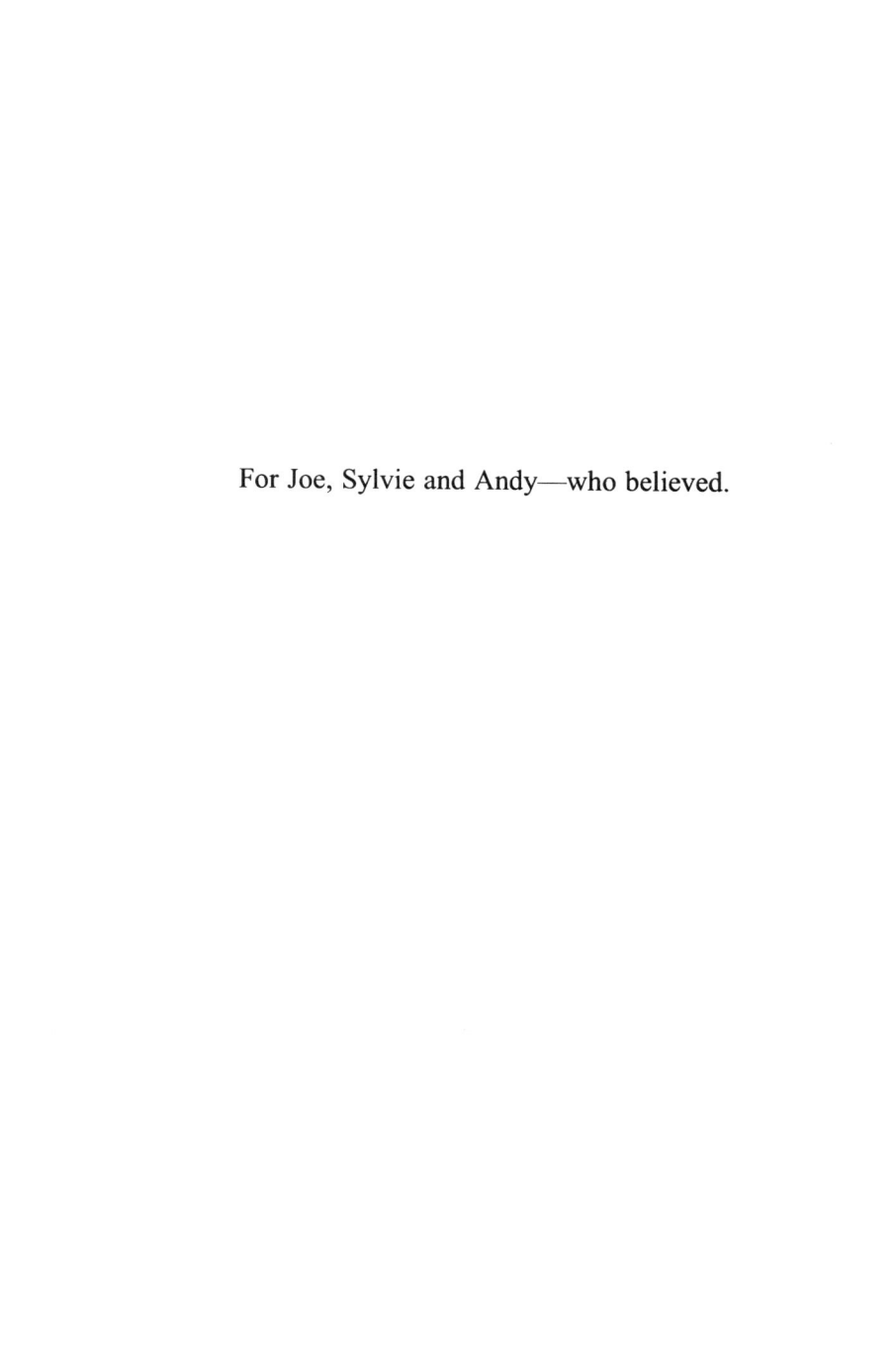

ACT ONE

SETTING: *The play is not literal, therefore, the scenery is not literal. Lighting provides for an uninterrupted flow of action and to allow jumps in time and space, as needed. There are three permanent features of the set: a Bed Area; a Farm Area and a Podium, all of which are used to suggest several locales and should not be too specific. The setting and special effects should never overshadow the words of EARL, as his rude, rural prose is the focus of the play.*

AT RISE: *In the dark we hear the VOICE of AUNTIE ALICE as she calls:*

ALICE. Li'l Earl? Li'l Earl? Come on home, boy!

(The lights rise on the Farm Area. AUNTIE ALICE is calling for young Earl. She looks off in the distance and speaks yearningly:)

Li'l Earl? You come when your Auntie Alice calls. Where are you, Li'l Earl? Is you lost? Where are you?

(The lights fade on her and rise on EARL at the Podium. It is a hot night. He douses a handkerchief with

Coca-Cola and swabs it on his face and neck to cool off.)

EARL. They say I'm a stripteaser. They say I'm a horse bettor. They say I'm a whiskey drinker. *(Pause.)* I might have done some of all of them. They say I stole the state of Louisiana. They haven't located it or found out where I put it yet—and they never will! *(He swabs again and rocks on his feet.)* I may be rough and tumble... You got to be rough sometimes. One of those namby-pamby hustlers in this race—how long would he last up here? About as long as a snowball in heaven.

(Don't correct the line. These, as is the case in most of the following speeches, are EARL's words. The apparent mistakes are his as he said them.)

There are some candidates in this race who are so selfish and self-centered they don't care if the poor, needy devils of this state go out and eat grass... They think the only people entitled to a college education are the blue bloods whose mothers, fathers, and grandfolks were born blue bloods, and the rest of the poor people shouldn't even have the right to breathe.

Now, out of a sorry bunch of candidates, I stand head and shoulders above them... You take old Delta Soup. You know who I mean. You tell that little sapsucker he's going to get beat as sure as he lives—and tell him I'm the man who invented rock-em-sock-em politics. I'm the last of the red-hot poppas in Louisiana politics.

Act I UNCLE EARL 11

(The lights fade on EARL and rise on BLANCHE, his wife, JOE ARTHUR, his aide, and a REPORTER for the Times-Picayune newspaper of New Orleans. A press conference of sorts is in progress.)

JOE. ...And you can tell the readers of the *Times-Picayune* that Uncle Earl has not yet committed to running for another term and is well aware of the constitutional difficulties involved. He is, at this point, just keeping his options open.
"TIMES-PICAYUNE." That's mighty fine, Joe Arthur, but he *sounds* like a candidate, and that is clearly against the law of the state of Louisiana...
JOE. There is nothing in the state constitution that says he can't SOUND like anything he wants to. There is, in the mind of the *Times-Picayune*, some little doubt as to whether or not Uncle Earl can succeed himself...
"TIMES-PICAYUNE." There is, in the mind of the *Times-Picayune* more than a little doubt as to whether or not Uncle Earl is, or ever was, fit to be governor in the first place...
BLANCHE. And what about you? What do you say?
"TIMES-PICAYUNE." Miz Blanche, I'm just a reporter...
BLANCHE. And I'm his wife. Now the publisher of the *Times-Picayune* is a long way away from me. You're standing right in front of me. What do *you* say?
"TIMES-PICAYUNE." About the governor, or about your husband?
BLANCHE. What difference is there?
"TIMES-PICAYUNE." "What difference is there?" That's something I hope you won't have to find out, Miz Blanche.

JOE. What you trying to say?

"TIMES-PICAYUNE." Uncle Earl's one hell of a man. And good copy. But he's riding a tiger on this one. I hope he don't end up inside. *(He starts to leave.)* Ma'am...

JOE. Why don't you speak up like a man if you want to say something?

BLANCHE. Joe Arthur... It's all right. *(To REPORTER.)* Thank you.

"TIMES-PICAYUNE." For what? *(He exits.)*

BLANCHE. Joe Arthur, we've got to be ready for trouble...

JOE. Aw, Miz Blanche, ain't nobody can hurt the governor...

BLANCHE. Anybody can be hurt, Joe Arthur. Especially in politics. You hear anybody saying things about Earl?

JOE. What kind of things, Miz Blanche?

BLANCHE. Things, Joe Arthur. The things that cut your life off with a whisper sharper than a knife...

JOE. People always been talking about Uncle Earl...

BLANCHE. They haven't always been saying what I hear they're saying now...

JOE. Don't pay people no mind, Miz Blanche. They can say what they want about the governor.

BLANCHE. They can say what they want about the governor, but not about my husband. Not about him. Not about me.

JOE. Now, Miz Blanche, if you been reading those stories about the governor hanging around them strip joints, that don't mean nothing. That's Uncle Earl blowing off steam...

Act I UNCLE EARL 13

BLANCHE. Don't be foolish, Joe Arthur. I know Earl. I know politics, too. I wasn't born to it, like he was, but I married into it and I know it about as well as anybody in the state.

JOE. Then, what you worried about, Miz Blanche?

BLANCHE. Responsibilities, Joe Arthur. I have a lot of them. To the state, to the family, to myself, and to Earl... I've got to balance them. But, most of all, if he's sick, I got to help him, Joe Arthur. I've got to do what's best for him...

JOE. Yes, ma'am...

BLANCHE. Is there anything you've noticed lately? Anything...?

JOE. Well, he's been worried about a lot of bills in the legislature and things. They coming up with a lot of segregation bills; there's a plan to purge the voter rolls... It's a hell of a time to be governor...

BLANCHE. Aren't we lucky, then, to have such a hell of a man...

(Lights fade on them and rise on EARL at the Podium.)

EARL. Sure I want to be governor... Only one person in 2,000,000 in this state can get to *be* governor... Think about that! Ain't that an honor? *(Eyes them roguishly.)* You live in the best house I ever lived in. You have servants. And you don't even have to buy your own food. Every time you open the door, someone hands you a ham or a turkey or a blanket or all that free stuff. Well, I *like* all that free stuff. *(Laughs with gusto.)* But let's get back to Delta Soup. I'd rather beat him than eat any blackberry or huckleberry pie my mama ever made. Oh, how I'm praying for that stump-wormer to get in there. I want him to roll up them cuffs, and get out that little tuppy (toupee) and make himself up. He's the kind of city slicker that uses that stuff under his arm... *(Mimes deodorant.)* Did you know he wears four-hundred-dollar suits?!... You put one of those four-hundred-dollar suits on Uncle Earl and it'd be like a rooster wearing socks! People say, "Why don't you debate him on television?"... Television makes me look like a monkey climbing a string...

But, I don't want to say any more about him. And I don't have to talk about me. You know me, and you knew my brother, Huey. You know I'm for the poor man; I'm for the farmer; I'm for the white man; I'm for the colored—that's right. I'm the first governor of this state to equalize the pay for white teachers and colored teachers... They do the same job, they should get the same pay... Sure, some of them complained, but I'm telling you right now, there are two groups you can't satisfy—prostitutes and teachers... But, a poor man is a poor man. It makes no difference what color he is. The law—like the veteran's bonus—is for everybody, including you colored folks who fought in the Army and the Navy. If the colored people helped build this country, if they could fight in its Army, they should vote. I'm for *anybody* who's got right on his side. You got to do right and be willing to take the heat for it. It ain't that I'm against stealin'...but it takes two of us to steal—and one of us might squeal...

If you want to check on a crook, check through another crook... If you ever take money from anyone, do it in the bathroom—with the door locked... And look behind the tub and the toilet first... *(Pauses.)* They were mad at me in St. Tammany because the last time I ran I promised them a road... But they didn't NEED it. I mean the traffic didn't justify the cost... So I had to be against it... Anyway, they were mad, "How come you promised us a road and now you won't build it?"... You know what I told them? I said, "I lied." But, I didn't. Because, all I ever promised in politics—and all I ever will promise—is to do right. That's it. That's all. Just, "Do right."

(EARL swabs again and walks to a seat at the rear. The lighting becomes mellower as he sits dousing and swabbing with his Coke. A young BOY carrying schoolbooks walks by the platform, looks around carefully, and spits on EARL's poster.)

EARL. What the hell you do that for, boy?
BOY. Who're you?
EARL. I'm the bogeyman and I want to know why you spitting in public? It ain't sanitary. You spreading germs.
BOY. Aw, you just supporting that redneck crook.
EARL. You mean Uncle Earl?
BOY. He ain't no uncle of mine.
EARL *(knowingly)*. Your daddy put you up to this...
BOY. What you want to know about my dad?
EARL. I know all I need to know. He ain't no friend to Uncle Earl.
BOY. He's gonna put him out of work.

EARL. Who is?

BOY *(points to poster)*. Him!

EARL. He don't put people out of work. He puts them *to* work...

BOY. Not my dad...

EARL *(light dawns)*. Your dad got a city job?

BOY. Yeah.

EARL. I see your problem... Well, I'm sorry, but I'm gonna have to have your name and address.

BOY. You gonna arrest me?

EARL. No, but I gotta report you. *(Points to poster.)* Like you said, he's an old redneck, and if I don't take care of business, he'd never forgive me.

BOY. He's mean, huh?

EARL. When he has to be, he's the meanest man who lived. Now, if I don't get your name and address, he's gonna give me fits tonight.

BOY. I don't want to get you in trouble. *(Points off to a house.)* I live there.

EARL. I see it.

BOY. I gotta go. *(Starts off.)*

EARL. Hey, son. *(BOY stops.)* Come back here. I won't bite. Less'n we in a fight. Lemme show you about politics... You see, you don't spit on people. Not in politics. Not in life. Makes bad feelings. But, what you can do is this... *(Stoops and picks up a handful of dirt.)* Throw a little dirt at them. If it sticks, they ain't no good. But, if they're good, it won't stick. Not permanent. *(Hands him dirt and points to the poster.)* Here. Try it. *(BOY takes dirt and starts to throw it. Looks at poster, then at EARL.)*

BOY. That's you.

EARL. Who?

BOY. Him. Him's you.

EARL. You think I'm that redneck crook?

BOY. Uh-huh.

EARL. They say he eats children for lunch. You think I eat children for lunch?

BOY. No. I don't know. *(Pause.)* You got kids?

EARL. No. *(Pause.)* No, I don't.

BOY. Why not?

EARL *(looks at him a moment)*. Ain't you gonna be late for school?

BOY. I guess. *(Pause.)* Can I go?

EARL. Who's gonna stop you?

BOY *(pause)*. 'Bye.

EARL. 'Bye. *(BOY runs off, EARL watches him go, then:)* Joe Arthur? Joe Arthur!

JOE *(entering)*. Yes, Uncle Earl?

EARL *(pointing)*. See who lives in that house over there. See he's got a job and that the family's OK.

JOE. Taking care of the needy at election time, eh?

EARL. He ain't needy. He's got what he needs. He's got a fine boy. See to it.

JOE *(starting off)*. Yes, Governor.

EARL. Joe Arthur!

JOE *(stops)*. Yes, Governor?

EARL. You know what I want when I die?

JOE. What, Governor?

EARL. I want to be buried in the middle of a playground. *(JOE laughs.)* I mean it. I never had no kids. Getting too old to expect any. If I can't be surrounded by kids in life, I'll have to settle for second best. I don't want to be stuck in front of that damn Capitol like my brother. I couldn't stand to be laying there and hear a lot of politicians swear to a pack of lies and me not being able to name them for the lying sons of bitches they know they are. *(Pause.)* See to it, Joe Arthur.

JOE. Yes, Uncle Earl... We got a few minutes before we have to get to the next stop. You want to go to the hotel and lie down?

EARL. Why'd I want to do that?

JOE. Miz Blanche made me promise to look after you. She's worried about your overdoing it. You had that heart attack...

EARL. I know I had a heart attack. I was there.

JOE. She's just worried about you.

EARL. Hell, yes. She don't want to lose her meal ticket.

JOE. Aw, you know how she feels...

EARL. I know how she feels...I was there. *(Pause.)* Lemme sit here for a while, Joe Arthur. Pick me up when it's time for the next stop.

JOE. OK, Uncle Earl...

(JOE leaves. EARL sits for a moment. The lights change. From offstage we hear:)

BILL. Earl! Hey, Earl!

(EARL stirs. The "dance theme" is heard and his memories come rushing back to him and we are caught up in them. BILL enters dressed in the style of the 1920s. Behind him, we can make out TWO GIRLS talking and the SOUNDS of a party.)

EARL. What do you want?

BILL. Come on, now, Earl. I'm trying to do you a favor. You can't spend all your time studying law. There's a good-looking little lady over here that I know you'd love to meet. *(He helps EARL spruce up.)* She's real smart and she's a real personable girl. A society girl.

EARL. Just what I need. An ex-traveling salesman, hill-country Baptist who's trying to sneak through a Catholic law school on a scholarship and you want to fix me up with a smart society girl.

BILL. Perfect. Between the two of you, you have everything.

EARL. I wouldn't know what to talk to her about.

BILL. Look, forget she's beautiful and smart and well-to-do. Let's say she works behind the cigar counter at the Monteleone Hotel. Walk up to her, buy some cigarettes, and pretend she's one of them damn "little people" you always go on about.

EARL. What a crazy idea...

BILL. Well, she just graduated from business college. Tell her you need a secretary. Hell, Earl, it's just a dance. What's she gonna matter. *(They have reached the chatting GIRLS.)* Earl, this is Blanche.

BLANCHE. Hello, Earl.

EARL *(stares at her a moment)*. You're gonna matter. You're gonna matter a lot.

BLANCHE. I beg your pardon?

EARL. I was just telling Bill here that I'd like to buy some cigarettes. *(They sweep into a dance.)*

BLANCHE. I understand you're a lawyer.

EARL. Not yet. I don't have a degree. Probably never have one in my life. But I know enough to pass the bar exams. Done most of my training at Loyola.

BLANCHE. You Catholic?

EARL. No, I'm Baptist.

BLANCHE. We're Methodist.

EARL. Well, Baptist, Catholic, Methodist... Lemme tell you about stuff like that. My mother was a rock-ribbed Baptist, but she was very, very tolerant and kind to all religions. When I was a child, we had six Catholics that boarded at our house, and my mother used to get up at five o'clock in the morning so these Catholics could go twenty miles in a surrey to church.

BLANCHE. Your mother must be quite a woman.

EARL. She's gone. I lost her when I was fourteen... I've heard a lot of people say they never knew a woman that was as tolerant as my mother. And I think we were more or less brought up that way. So, really and truly, religion or creed or color doesn't make any difference to me.

BLANCHE. That was young to lose your mother.

EARL. Well, I had a lot of sisters. Schoolteachers. So I was well brought up. But my mama set us on the path. *(He clears his throat, a rasping, racking cough.)*

BLANCHE. Do you have a cold?

EARL. No. When I was five I accidentally drank some lye. It didn't kill me, but Enrico Caruso never had to fear for his job. I'm a little beat up, I guess...

BLANCHE. "Bloody, but unbowed..."

EARL. You know Huey's poem?

BLANCHE. Huey didn't write "Invictus."

EARL. Might as well have...

BLANCHE. So you're a lawyer...

EARL. So you're a secretary...

BLANCHE. What do you like to read?

EARL. Why?

BLANCHE. Making talk.
EARL. Grocery ads.
BLANCHE. Grocery ads?
EARL. I can't resist bargains. It's the way I was brought up.
BLANCHE. Anything else?
EARL. I read the newspapers. Even though they lie a lot. The Bible. I know a lot of that by heart... Huey's the intellectual. He gets up to talk and for the first couple of minutes you don't know what he's talking about. He wants the intellectuals to know he's one of them... I can't do that. I got a good vocabulary, but I don't see anything wrong with talking so the poorest farmer can understand you... You know, I'm always gonna remember you as you are right now...
BLANCHE. Right now?
EARL. Right now.
BLANCHE. And how long is "always"?
EARL. We'll see, won't we? *(His intensity unsettles her.)*
BLANCHE. Tell me about your famous brother.
EARL. You know about Huey.
BLANCHE. EVERYBODY knows about HUEY. Tell me about Earl's famous brother...

(As EARL speaks he drifts away and BLANCHE is lost in the dark. He moves to the Podium.)

EARL. I ain't like Huey. He can go chargin' around and get away with it. I've gotta go slower. Huey can't go straight at things. He's got to corkscrew around for the fun of it. When he built the new Charity Hospital in New Orleans, a colored preacher come to see him to complain they weren't no colored nurses in there. So Huey told him he would get jobs for the colored nurses. The reverend might not like the *way* he got them jobs, but they'd get the jobs. He toured the hospital and came out and held a press conference...

(He is now at the Podium. He imitates Huey's fist-pounding delivery.)

It's a disgrace. It's a gawdamned disgrace and I won't put up with it. I took a tour of that hospital, and I saw women—fine Southern women—nurses—and they were forced to cater to and take care of colored patients. Now that's a disgrace and I will not have it. Starting tomorrow, I'm gonna have COLORED nurses in there to take care of the colored patients. You can tell your readers the Kingfish said it and it WILL be done... *(Shrugs.)* The colored nurses got the jobs... *(He looks around.)* Huey? Blanche?

(He sits at the rear of the podium where JOE left him. The "dance theme" is heard faintly. From off comes the sound of JOE's VOICE.)

JOE. Uncle Earl?
EARL. What?
JOE *(entering)*. Time to get to the next speech.
EARL. I must have dozed. I was dreaming...
JOE. You getting tired?
EARL. Maybe...
JOE. We can wait. We don't have to do this right now...
EARL. 'Course we do. You wanna stop?

JOE. I want to do whatever you want to do, Uncle Earl. You know that.
EARL. You a good man, Joe Arthur. I don't know what I'd do without you.
JOE. Thank you, Uncle Earl.
EARL. You welcome. Sometimes I wonder why you put up with me.
JOE. So do I, Uncle Earl.
EARL. Yeah. It don't look like there's gonna be much in it for you.
JOE. I'm not complaining. *(EARL nods off.)* You feel tired?
EARL. No. Just old. But not dead. Don't look so worried, Joe Arthur. I got a lot of kicking to do before I'm ready to go home. Let's get to that next speech. *(EARL exits. JOE watches uncertainly as the "dance theme" plays.)*
JOE. We can hold off if you feel tired... I'll call ahead, Uncle Earl. They'll wait. Yeah, they'll wait. Of course, they'll wait. Who the hell wouldn't wait a few extra minutes to see one of the Seven Wonders of the World...

(Lights and music fade out as JOE starts off. In the dark, TROOPER CRAWFORD [CRAWDADDY], a state policeman, enters with a flashlight. He is "making rounds." He yawns, stretches, and with a shake of his head, sits for a moment, dozing in the night as the lights build. EARL enters in his BVDs. "CRAWDADDY" jumps to his feet as he becomes aware of EARL.)

"CRAWDADDY." Who's there?
EARL. I'm here. Who and what the hell are you?

"CRAWDADDY." Trooper Crawford, sir.

EARL. And what you doing here, Crawfish?

"CRAWDADDY." I'm the night guard, Governor.

EARL. Doing a good job, too, I can see.

"CRAWDADDY." I'm sorry, Governor. I dozed off a little.

EARL. You're luckier than I am. I been trying to sleep and I can't. Miz Blanche is down in New Orleans…I just ain't comfortable alone. *("CRAWDADDY" yawns.)* I keeping you awake, son?

"CRAWDADDY." Sorry, Governor. I just switched over to this night shift. I been working days and my youngest been keeping us up nights and I'm a little short of sleep.

EARL. You got kids?

"CRAWDADDY." Yes, sir.

EARL. How many?

"CRAWDADDY." Three.

EARL. Well. You ain't a crawFISH you a crawDADDY. I wisht I was.

"CRAWDADDY." What, Governor?

EARL. A daddy. You a lucky man, Crawdaddy.

"CRAWDADDY." I think so. Kids wear you out, but… well, they keep you going, too.

EARL. We ain't got none. Always wanted some. Got me a fine wife. She's pretty. She's educated. She's smart. She's got ambitions—all kinds of ambitions. She wants to be known as the best-dressed woman in Baton Rouge. The most intelligent. The best of everything. *("CRAWDADDY" yawns again.)* There's a few things she don't like… She don't like to go up to my pea patch farm; she don't like my cussing and spitting… I don't like my cussing, but I don't drink anymore and a man's got to have *some* failing... As for spitting... Well, I'm country, she's city... *("CRAWDADDY" yawns again. EARL sees him.)* One other thing she don't like is me sleeping in my BVDs on the porch, but *I* like it. It's the best sleeping there is. *(Helps "CRAWDADDY" up.)* Now, you go into that nice air-conditioned bedroom of mine and catch up on your sleep so you can be a Daddy Crawdaddy to your young'uns. Just bring me some coffee at six o'clock in the morning.

"CRAWDADDY." But, Governor, I'm on guard. I got to guard you. I could get fired.

EARL. Well, if it come to that, I just might be able to save your job, Trooper Crawdaddy.

"CRAWDADDY." But, I got to protect you...

EARL. Now, who the hell would want to hurt Uncle Earl? Good night, son.

"CRAWDADDY." Good night, Governor... *("CRAWDADDY" leaves and EARL settles himself for the night. Phone rings.)*

EARL. Hello.

(The lights rise on the other side of the stage to reveal BLANCHE on the phone.)

BLANCHE. Earl? I was afraid you were still up. Are you sick?

EARL. Naw, I'm all right. Just antsy.

BLANCHE. What's the matter?

EARL. That damn *Times-Picayune*.

BLANCHE. Oh.

EARL. Yeah. "Oh." They out telling everybody what an ugly old man Uncle Earl is. I don't mind them criticizing me when I'm wrong, but I'd sure like a fair shake of the dice when I'm right.

BLANCHE. They're against the tax increase?

EARL. What the hell they ever for, except the fat cats? A drunk *Times-Picayune* reporter was stumbling down the street and he fell into the gutter. A little while later a pig came along and sat down next to him. Soon, a little old lady passed by and she said, "You can certainly know someone by the company he keeps." The pig got up and walked away.

BLANCHE. You're practicing on me, aren't you?

EARL. Some. What you think?

BLANCHE. Not bad. Why don't you add, "He was right, too. He was an honest pig."

EARL. OK. Sounds good. Too bad I can't say it about the publisher. I LIKE reporters.

BLANCHE. You watch your tongue when I'm not there to do it for you.

EARL. Hmmph. I expect you're telling everyone you really run things.

BLANCHE. I only tell the truth.

EARL. I should never have made you National Democratic Committeewoman.

BLANCHE. Oh? I thought I earned that on my own?

EARL. You deciding you want to wear the pants, Miz Blanche? You been spending too much time in "society"?

BLANCHE. I'm just being a good secretary...who's more than a little in love with her boss. *(Pause.)* You go to sleep. You have to watch your health.

EARL. I'm gonna have to watch more than that...

BLANCHE. What does that mean?

EARL. I mean that there are some pinheads in that zoo of a legislature that are up to no good. Your New Orleans society friends you like so much are pushing the idea they should review the voter rolls. They CLAIM the idea is to remove deceased and unqualified and non-voting registrants. Hell, they think my mama raised stupid sons? They want to clear the rolls all right. They wanna clear them of Uncle Earl's voters! That's the idea. All them old people who vote for Uncle Earl because he gets them a few dollars more for welfare... All them nigra voters who always vote for Earl because he sees they get a fair shake in life... They scared I'm gonna run again. And they sure as hell don't want to see Uncle Earl back here, because they know damn well there ain't no way they could tell me what to do.

BLANCHE. I worry when I hear you talk that way... You should be asleep. You need to rest. I thought you'd be in bed.

EARL. If you thought I'd be in bed, why'd you call?

BLANCHE. Well, I HOPED you'd be... What are you doing this weekend?

EARL. I thought I'd take a few boys to the pea patch.

BLANCHE. Then, I am most certainly *not* coming home.

EARL. It figures. *(Laughs.)* They been setting up the Attorney General. Joe Arthur's been telling him what a palace my billy-goat ranch is. I can't wait to see old Jack's face. *(Both laugh.)* We'll get there at night, and in the morning he'll see Ole Earl's big ole ranch for himself.

BLANCHE. That's almost worth the trip.

EARL. Wanna come?

BLANCHE. Positively not.

EARL. Why'd I marry you, anyway?

BLANCHE. You needed a pack of cigarettes.
EARL. Good night, queen of Mardi Gras...
BLANCHE. Good night...

(The lights fade on them. In the dark, we hear a ROOSTER crow. When the lights rise on the Farm Area, we see EARL in his BVDs. The ATTORNEY GENERAL is in pants, suspenders and undershirt. He is barefoot.)

ATTORNEY GENERAL. Morning, Governor.
EARL. Morning, hell! It's the middle of the day.
ATTORNEY GENERAL. What time is it?
EARL. Eight-thirty.
ATTORNEY GENERAL. Breakfast ready?
EARL. It was at five o'clock when I got up... I guess Sadie can fix you up. Want some eggs?
ATTORNEY GENERAL. That'd be nice.
EARL. Fine. You'll find all the eggs you want out in the barn. Go gather up how many you want to eat and give 'em to Sadie and she'll cook them up for you.
ATTORNEY GENERAL. The barn?
EARL. Out back. *(Picks up his newspaper. The ATTORNEY GENERAL stands waiting.)* Anything the matter?
ATTORNEY GENERAL. Nothing.
EARL. Good. Go get your breakfast.

(The ATTORNEY GENERAL wanders off. Silence. EARL reads his paper. From outside we hear a few tentative "Chick-chicks," then a terrible clatter and clucking. A few feathers drift in as EARL looks up. With further banging, SADIE, a handsome black woman, enters.)

SADIE. Mr. Earl, I'll do it, but he can't.
EARL. You-will-he-can't-what?
SADIE. I'll fix his eggs, but he can't come inside and that's all there is to it.
EARL. He's the attorney general of the state of Louisiana, the top lawyer in the state. Why can't he come inside?
SADIE. He may know law, but he don't know nothin' 'bout barns. He done fell in the yard and he covered with chicken mess. He can't come in my house.
EARL. Well, tell him rich, white people eat on the patio and he can, too.
SADIE. We ain't got no patio.
EARL. Then tell him to sit outside the chicken coop.
SADIE. Yes, sir, Mr. Earl...

(As she goes grumbling off, the light fades and EARL muses:)

EARL. I wonder if the publisher of the *Times-Picayune* would like to come up and gather eggs with the Attorney General next week? I sure would like to see that sapsucker hunting his breakfast...

(There is laughter in the dark. When the lights rise, we see the ATTORNEY GENERAL, JOE and BILL playing cards.)

ATTORNEY GENERAL. You might have warned me...
BILL. And let you miss the baptism of fire?
ATTORNEY GENERAL. I've been baptized before, you know. The first time, all they used was water.
JOE. Well, now you know the pea patch.

ATTORNEY GENERAL. I don't know why I didn't expect it.

BILL. The thing is, Uncle Earl is who he IS. That's what the voters see and that's what they vote for. I guess he's about as true to himself as anybody I ever heard of.

ATTORNEY GENERAL. I can testify that Earl has got the soil of Louisiana under his feet. If that was all that got under my feet, and in my hair and up my nose I would've been a much happier man.

BILL. Everybody's got an Uncle Earl story.

JOE. Right, I remember the time, late one night, he had some business to take care of so I gave him a call. Him and Miz Blanche were in a hotel and Miz Blanche was sleeping...

(The lights fade as he speaks and rise on the Bed Area. MIZ BLANCHE is sleeping. EARL, wearing his BVDs, speaks in a stage whisper on the phone.)

EARL. No, dammit, I can't talk no louder. Miz Blanche is sleeping... I said, "Miz Blanche is sleeping"... Good God. Where are you? I'll call on another line... Where?... All right.

BLANCHE *(waking)*. Earl? That you?

EARL. Yeah, honey, go back to sleep. I got to call Joe Arthur. I'll use another line. *(He leaves.)*

BLANCHE *(after a moment, she sits up)*. Earl? Where are you going to find another phone? We're on the twentieth floor of the hotel. *(Picks up his trousers.)* My God! What did you go out of here wearing?

(Blackout. Lights rise on EARL on the phone in his BVDs.)

EARL. Joe Arthur? That you, Joe Arthur?... Good. Now I left Miz Blanche sleeping so I could cuss and raise hell without waking her. What the hell does that little sapsucker think he's doing?... Oh, he does, does he? Well, you tell him that when I say "Go" he goes and when I say "Stop" he stops and if I tell him to piddle I want to see a puddle spread... What?

(TWO PARTYGOERS enter carrying glasses, a bottle and noisemakers. They stare at EARL.)

EARL. That's because I'm out politicking while the others are sleeping... The only ones they got a majority of are liars and hypocrites and I'm willing to let them have a majority of those... *(Sees PARTYGOERS.)* Evening, folks.

FIRST PARTYGOER. Evening, Governor...

EARL. Naw, I don't need no five thousand dollars to endorse him. I only asked for it because I knew he was as tight as a tick's navel and I wanted to sweat him a little... All right. Be there tomorrow. *(To PARTYGOERS.)* Y'all have a good night, hear? *(EARL exits. The PARTYGOERS look at each other and toss their bottle in the trash can.)*

SECOND PARTYGOER. Last drop I'll ever drink...

(Lights black out and rise on card game. JOE, BILL and the ATTORNEY GENERAL laugh.)

ATTORNEY GENERAL. That's Earl. That's Earl!

BILL. Ain't no telling what he'll do. You ever been on one of his shopping trips? We were on our way to the Capitol and were outside Krotz Springs, oh, I suppose it was about two a.m., but, then, Earl always did make his own hours. Anyway he told the chauffeur to pull off the road into this farmyard...

(As he speaks, the lights fade and rise on the Farm Area. EARL enters, followed by the "CRAWDADDY," the "TIMES-PICAYUNE," and BILL with a flashlight. They tiptoe and whisper.)

BILL. Earl, are you sure this is a good idea? There's not a light on in the house.

EARL. Well, hell, these people have to be up in three hours to do their chores. You don't expect them to be out here with a band to meet us, do you? Ain't no use waking them. I already paid for the chickens. We'll just take them and go.

BILL. I can't see my foot or my fanny...

"CRAWDADDY." Uh, that's not YOUR fanny, Senator...

BILL. Sorry, Trooper...

EARL. You let Crawdaddy alone. Head over to the right...

"TIMES-PICAYUNE." Governor, where *is* the henhouse?

EARL. I don't rightly know...

"TIMES-PICAYUNE." But you HAVE been here before?

EARL. Well, not at this time of night. Who the hell would go visiting at this time of night? Now, Crawdaddy, *(Sending out the troops.)* you go around the back...

"CRAWDADDY." What am I looking for, Uncle Earl?

EARL. If it's got feathers, you call out. But, if it quacks, keep going. Times-Picayune, you go down there. We'll head off yonder. *(They leave.)*
BILL. What you want me to do, Earl?
EARL. If I was you, I'd turn that flashlight off. Somebody was to see it shining in the dark they could get the wrong idea.

(BILL hastily flicks off the light. The stage is momentarily dark, then there is a clatter of pails and a scream followed by the ear-splitting cackle of extremely perturbed chickens and a shotgun blast.)

VOICE. Who's out thar with my chickens?
EARL. Damn, I shoulda known better than to bring city boys along. Don't shoot, it's Uncle Earl. I come for my chickens.

(The ear-splitting cackle of extremely perturbed chickens continues along with yelling from EARL'S RAIDERS. At the height of the racket, the lights come up on the card game.)

BILL. There we were, sneaking around like the National Guard on bivouac and all of a sudden chickens are squawking, and shotguns are firing. It seems the farmer took umbrage at a raid on his chicken coop...
JOE. You get the chickens?
BILL. Of course we got the chickens. Farmer loaded them in the limousine himself when he found out it was Earl. THEN he wanted to stop somewhere for watermelon...
ATTORNEY GENERAL. Can't imagine Huey doing that.

BILL. Huey was a different animal. Earl was the organization man and Huey had the vision.
ATTORNEY GENERAL. Huey used to buy the legislature like a sack of potatoes.
JOE. Uncle Earl said he never bought a legislature in his life.
BILL. Naw, he just rents them.
ATTORNEY GENERAL. Cheaper that way...
JOE. He's gonna have some problems with *this* legislature...
BILL. Uncle Earl's riding the tiger for sure...
ATTORNEY GENERAL. And you know where he's liable to end up...
JOE. You can't expect him to swallow that segregation stuff. It's not the way he was raised. It's not the way him and Huey done business all their lives.
BILL. If I recall, Huey didn't have all that long a life...
ATTORNEY GENERAL. Remember what he said before he died?
JOE. "God, don't let me die. I got so much to do..."

(He taps the table for luck. BILL and the ATTORNEY GENERAL do the same. Their tapping builds in rhythm as the lights fade and SEGUES into the SOUND OF GUNFIRE which SEGUES in turn to THUNDER. In the dark we hear:)

EARL. "God, don't let me die. I got so much to do..."

(There is another CLAP OF THUNDER which SEGUES to JOE KNOCKING. Lights rise on EARL in bed.)

JOE. Uncle Earl? You in there? You all right?

(EARL sits up in bed as JOE enters.)

EARL. What?
JOE. I thought I heard you call out. You have a dream?
EARL. I been doing a lot of dreaming, Joe Arthur. And thinking. About things, and me, and...Huey. Something's gonna happen, Joe Arthur...
JOE. What, Uncle Earl? You worried about getting shot? Like Huey?
EARL. Huh? Naw. But there's lots of ways to skin a cat without stuffing him with butter.
JOE. What's that mean, Uncle Earl?
EARL. It means we got to get back to the capital tomorrow. They gonna try to purge the voter rolls this week. They can't get at me square and fair, so they gonna try to take the vote away from a lot of people—black and white—that they know'll vote for me. They gonna try to shoot me down just like they shot Huey. They just trying to use a different kind of bullet.
JOE. At least you can't get hurt with these.
EARL. You can always get hurt, Joe Arthur. Some hurts just last a little longer and hurt a little deeper. Go to bed, we going back tomorrow. Be ready for a hell of a fight. No, sir. It ain't over yet...

(Picked out briefly in a spot, AUNTIE ALICE calls:)

ALICE. Li'l Earl? Come on home, boy. Come on home...

(The lights rise on BLANCHE at the DL phone. She picks up the phone and puts it down twice. The third time, she dials the operator.)

BLANCHE. Operator? I'd like the number of the Sealy Psychiatric Hospital in Galveston, Texas... Yes, I'll hold...

(She presses a handkerchief to lips. Her face contorts in a silent sob. The lights fade. In the dark we hear the SOUND OF SIRENS and SCUFFLING. In dim light we can make out THREE FIGURES. One of them is EARL and he is furious.)

NURSE. Look out for him. He bites.
EARL. Get your damn hands off me!
ORDERLY. Grab his arm! Look out for his teeth! Dammit. He bit me!
EARL. Who's in charge? Who's in charge here?
NURSE. Governor, we don't want to hurt you. This is for your own good!
EARL. You got a damn funny way of showing me what's good for me. Who's in charge? You in charge? Dammit, when a man's being kidnapped he's got a right to know who's running the show! *(Lights rise on EARL.)* Joe Arthur! Joe Arthur! Where the hell are you, Joe Arthur? *(EARL picks up a microphone for a tape recorder.)* This is Uncle Earl, your governor, talking to you from Sealy Hospital in Galveston. 'Course you know I've gone through quite a bit in the last three or four weeks... These people opposed to the loan-shark bill have conspired with my wife, who is one of the most jealous

women God ever let live on this Earth—and, really and truly she has very little to be jealous about...

(Lights rise on another area where the DOCTOR, PSYCHOLOGIST and BLANCHE sit around a table.)

DOCTOR. And, this...behavior began after he returned from the farm?

BLANCHE. I knew this was coming eight months ago, it was just as plain as day. Suddenly Earl started talking about running for a fourth term as governor and it got so that that was all he would talk about. He stopped eating, and, even though he had given up smoking because he had a thrombosis condition, he started to smoke cigarettes again. He began to drive himself unmercifully...

EARL. If I'm nuts, then I've always been nuts. I don't want a dog or a poor man or any man—black or white—to be subjected to the abuse I've gone through. *(He breaks into a coughing spell.)* This is Uncle Earl, governor-in-exile by force and kidnapping... *(Coughing spell again.)* Joe Arthur? Joe Arthur? Where the hell are you, Joe Arthur? *(Lights fade on EARL.)*

BLANCHE. After a long day at the Capitol, he would come home and go to bed. But he couldn't sleep. After an hour or two of tossing and turning, he would get up and walk around the bedroom or, perhaps, sit up in a chair with a light on... I was so sick with worry over him that I called the family together and warned them that we would have to do something or Earl would drive himself into the grave...

(The DOCTOR and PSYCHOLOGIST consult gravely for a moment.)

DOCTOR. It is our opinion that the governor suffered a series of light strokes prior to coming to the hospital here. His physical condition was such that he could not stand the terrific pace he set for himself...
PSYCHOLOGIST. It is very conceivable that the numerous small strokes that the governor apparently did suffer could have brought about a change in personality accounting for the symptoms which he had... He has been behaving strangely, you say...
BLANCHE. Yes. There were...incidents...

(The lights fade on the scene and rise on the "TIMES-PICAYUNE" on the phone.)

"TIMES-PICAYUNE." OK. I'm on a phone line at the Capitol. Uncle Earl is expected any moment to address a hostile legislature out to thwart his plans...

(EARL enters, carrying a bottle of Coke which has been "doctored.")

EARL. Hell's bells, the press. You still shilling for that silk-stocking, sweet-smelling, dirty-dealing *Times-Picayune*?
"TIMES-PICAYUNE." That's what it says on the paycheck...
EARL. I suppose you'll be behind that fancy, slick-as-a-peeled-onion mayor of yours in the next election.
"TIMES-PICAYUNE." I write the news. I don't make it.

Act I UNCLE EARL 39

EARL. You're not looking so well. What's your trouble?
"TIMES-PICAYUNE." Nothing, Uncle Earl. Just a sore throat.
EARL. I can't have you getting sick. You get sick and they might send one of them Tulane graduates up here. *(Offers bottle.)* Here. Take a swig of this. *("TIMES-PICAYUNE" takes a healthy slug, goes into a violent fit of coughing.)* Anything the matter?
"TIMES-PICAYUNE." Nothing. Just not used to one-hundred-proof Coke.
EARL. It is the pause that refreshes, you know...

(The lights black out on them and change to reveal BLANCHE, JOE and the ATTORNEY GENERAL trying to restrain BILL.)

BLANCHE. Please, Bill, please.
JOE. Hey, come on, now, buddy. You know Earl...
BILL. I won't have it. I'm sorry. I won't have it. No man can use language like that in front of my wife. Not while I'm around.
ATTORNEY GENERAL. Bill, you've been with Earl as long and as close as anybody in the state...
BILL. And I've been loyal to him, too.
BLANCHE. Bill, Earl has a good heart. You know that. And you know his language can be... Well, Lord knows I've tried to get him to... Bill, is it really worth a split?
BILL. I'm afraid so, Miz Blanche.
JOE. Earl needs friends. He's facing a rough time.
BILL. It's going to get rougher. I know I'm a bit of a prude, but there's nobody going to yell four-letter words

in my wife's presence without me calling him on it... Governor or no.

ATTORNEY GENERAL. Bill, I think this can be worked out. Earl's tired. He's not well...

BILL. He spit on me, General. He spit on me in public. He told me to go to hell. In front of my wife. He told me to go to hell to my face...and I lost face.

JOE. What about a vacation and a new state job?

BILL. I am through with Earl. It's over... Goodbye, all. *(Exits.)*

BLANCHE. What are we going to do? What are we going to do?

JOE. Uncle Earl is due to address the legislature. We better get there.

(Lights rise on the Podium Area. There is a buzz of noise. EARL appears, swigs from his Coke and goes to Podium and stands, swaying, surveying the legislature. When he has their attention he speaks, ruminatively at first, then building in intensity.)

EARL. About 1908, I had an uncle who got killed... He'd been a good man... Good to his family... Good to me... He taught me to ride a horse... Well... He got drunk one night...went down to the colored quarter...where a nigra man was in bed with his wife, kicked that nigra man out of bed...and he got into that bed. That nigra man was so enraged, he shot my poor uncle and he died. There are too many people around who sleep with nigras at night...and kick them in the daytime. *(A discontented rumble comes from his audience.)* Now, everybody's all worked up about segregation. There's a whole hopper of segregation bills. I don't see any need to pass a whole lot of segregation bills, even though I would favor them, when the U.S. Supreme Court probably would knock them out anyway.

There are important things to be done in this state. There's the loan-shark bill to pass. There's highways that need fixing; and I think this segregation stuff is an attempt by the people who *have* to throw sand in your eyes so they can keep it and not spread it around to the people in this state who are needy.

All this carrying on is nothing but the NAAPC (Not a typographical error, just Earl.) and a few pin-headed nuts in this legislature playing "you-goose-me-and-I'll-goose-you." But, I'll say this...one day when this body ain't in session, them people will probably go home, take off their shoes, wash their feet, look up at the moon, and get close to God. And when you do, you got to realize that nigras is human beings... That's something that Wee Willie and his pin-headed pecans just can't seem to realize. All they seem to have time to do is dream up more and more outlandish laws that spit on the Constitution of the United States... *(Another discontented rumble comes from his audience.)* Oh, sure, I signed some of his bills into law. You either sign bills like that or you go to the North Pole. Fellas like him or Governor Faubus want to go behind Lincoln—and, between us, gentleman, we got to admit that Lincoln was a fine man and that he was right...Republican or no Republican. There are good Republicans. Eisenhower—a good man and honest—of course, he's a misfit. It's a wonder Eisenhower has done as well as he has, knowing as little as he does about government... But I ain't never voted for the Republican ticket in my life. The Republicans are for the rich man. *(He stops to take a drink from his bottle.)* I don't need this job. I don't need money. I don't miss it—unless I run out. I got a deal with the Lord. I don't care nothing about money... If I go where I hope I'm going, I won't need any. If I go to the other place, it'll burn.

But, there's people doing business—right in this hall. Oh, yes... You know the rules of politics: don't write what you can say; don't say what you can smile; don't smile what you can nod; don't nod what you can wink!

Oh, yeah! You gotta be careful. Two things a man should never do—put money in a bank and write to a woman... You know what they say, "Do right and fear no man; don't write and fear no woman."

Oh, yeah! This is a fine legislature, isn't it?... This is the best legislature money can buy... The Bible says that before the end of time, all the pussycats, the poodle dogs, the house cats, and the lions and tigers are all going to lie down and sleep together... When I look at some of the gang in this room, it looks like the end of time is here already... *(A wave of hostile noise breaks over his head.)* We got the finest roads, finest hospitals, finest schools in the country—yet there are rich men who complain. They sit there swallowin' hundred-dollar bills like a bullfrog swallows minners (minnows) —if you chunked 'em as many as they wanted, they'd bust.

But still the *Picayune* says they don't know; they can't understand...well, there's a hell of a lot that they don't understand that they *do* understand, but they don't want *you* to understand. And as long as I've got the breath and the life and the health, I've got the fortitude and the backbone to tell 'em—and, dammit, they *know* I'll tell 'em—and that's why they're against me.

(Lights fade on EARL and the "dance theme" builds. In the dark, we hear BLANCHE. As she speaks, the lights build to reveal her with the DOCTOR and PSYCHOLOGIST as before.)

BLANCHE. So...because of all this, and on the advice of...friends...I felt it was duty as a wife to assure him of this chance of full recovery.
PSYCHOLOGIST. Rest assured. You did the right thing for him.
BLANCHE. I sincerely pray that, when he is well, he will feel the family has done the only thing possible under the circumstances...
PSYCHOLOGIST. I'm sure everyone feels that way...
BLANCHE. I wish I could be so sure... What do *you* think is wrong with Earl?
PSYCHOLOGIST. In my examination I formed the opinion that the governor is suffering from delusions of persecution which are "fixed."
BLANCHE. What exactly does that mean?
PSYCHOLOGIST. It's hard to put these matters in layman's terms. He would fit into the diagnostic category of paranoid schizophrenia with cycles of manic depressive activity... Can you understand that?

BLANCHE. I suppose. I'm feeling a little depressed myself...

(Lights fade and rise on EARL in his hospital bed. There is a suggestion of screening in the lights.)

EARL. Joe Arthur? Joe Arthur? Where the hell are you, Joe Arthur?

(The DOCTOR appears in a pool of light.)

DOCTOR. I had no idea the governor was coming as an uncooperative patient. I had been assured that his arrival was entirely voluntary. I must say I think on this score I was deceived. *(The DOCTOR moves to EARL.)*
EARL. I can't keep my mouth shut. It'd take an act of God to shut me up.
DOCTOR. Governor, if we could just calm down for a minute...
EARL. This ain't no hospital. This is a nuthouse. I heard what they call this wing—"Psycho Two."
DOCTOR. That's a nickname patients aren't supposed to hear. That orderly will be disciplined...
EARL *(points to screening)*. What the hell is that? An animal cage?
DOCTOR. We think bars have an unfortunate effect on patients, so we use the screening.
EARL. Why, if a man tried to escape through one of those screens, he'd leave his brains hanging on it.
DOCTOR. Governor, I don't want to jump to any conclusions. I want you to be assured that I am here to help you and that I am on your side.

EARL. I need *somebody* on my side and that's for damn sure. I've been kept a prisoner in the State Mansion; manhandled by bonecrushers from Mandeville and shot full of dope like a pincushion; and dragged off to Galveston; and, if you want me to do one damn thing, you'd better start by saying that I ain't getting no more needles stuck in my behind.
DOCTOR. Governor, if you'll cooperate, there'll be no more needles.
EARL. Doc, you've got yourself a deal. *(Offers hand. They shake.)*
DOCTOR. Now, Governor, you need a few days' rest. I want you to sleep, eat, and stay off the phone. No business. And no whiskey.
EARL. That'd suit me fine.

(EARL leaves. The PSYCHOLOGIST enters watching him.)

DOCTOR. Interesting case.
PSYCHOLOGIST. Obviously a paranoid schizophrenic.
DOCTOR. I'm afraid I can't agree.
PSYCHOLOGIST. And may I ask why?
DOCTOR. I'm convinced the problem is organic.
PSYCHOLOGIST. No, no. A deep-seated neurosis.
DOCTOR. The physical symptoms mitigate against that.
PSYCHOLOGIST. Can you isolate this alleged condition?
DOCTOR. Not at this time. Can you identify the causative event of your diagnosis?
PSYCHOLOGIST. Not at this time. *(They glare at each other a moment. A truce is called.)*

DOCTOR. Well. We have time. The patient is under control...

(The lights fade and rise on the Bed Area. EARL is on the phone. He is playing cards with "CRAWDADDY" and the NURSE. They are drinking bourbon and smoking cigars. From time to time EARL will grab a puff or a slug between snatches of his phone conversations. LUCILLE, Earl's sister, bustles around, emptying ashtrays and cleaning glasses. She places plates of food before the men.)

EARL. I don't care what the damn doctor said... He said you should run the state... That you wouldn't be hearing from me for a while... Well, he's a smart man... Now, you decide how smart you're gonna be. You decide whether you're gonna listen to him or me. You got about five seconds...

"CRAWDADDY." How many cards?

NURSE. Two for me.

EARL *(nods with satisfaction)*. Good. Now, like I said, fire the SOB... *(Another phone rings.)* Hold on a second... *(Answers other phone.)* Earl-in-exile... Yeah... No... Well, give him a job... *(Hangs up. Back to the first phone.)*

LUCILLE *(to NURSE)*. For heaven's sake, use a coaster...

EARL. Yeah... Well, don't listen to him... *(A third phone rings.)* Hold on...

"CRAWDADDY." Could I have another ashtray?

LUCILLE. It's a nasty habit...

"CRAWDADDY" *(to NURSE)*. Want a drink? *(She grabs the bottle and chug-a-lugs.)*

EARL *(picks up phone)*. Hello... What radio station?... I suppose so... Wait a second... *(First phone.)* See if he's in his office... Naw, I'll hang on... Some radio station is interviewing me on the other line...

LUCILLE. Get you a glass, dear?

NURSE. No, thanks.

LUCILLE. Maybe a trough?

EARL *(second phone)*. All right. You can go ahead, now... *(Third phone rings. "CRAWDADDY" answers. EARL continues on second phone.)* Well, I can think of ways I'd rather see Texas than through steel mesh.

"CRAWDADDY." Hold on. I'll see...

EARL. Naw, why should I blame the state of Texas... *(First phone.)* You there yet? *(Second phone.)* No, I'm holding another call...

"CRAWDADDY." Governor, you want anything in the third race?

EARL *(into phone)*. Wait a second. I got a question on state business... *(To "CRAWDADDY.")* Who's running? *(Second phone.)* What's your next question? *(First phone.)* You know I can't tie up this phone all day while you scratch your fanny...

DOCTOR *(enters)*. Governor, what's happening here? Who are these people? What are these phones? What are you doing?

EARL *(into each phone in turn)*. Call you back. Interview's over. Bet to show. *(To DOCTOR.)* Evening, Doc. *(LUCILLE puts a plate in front of EARL.)* Catfish, mustard greens, and huckleberry pie. Meet my sister. She came to cook for me.

(Blackout. Lights rise on PSYCHOLOGIST. The DOCTOR enters into the scene.)

PSYCHOLOGIST. The way he acts most of the time is beyond belief. If you tried to write a script about it and sell it to a TV show, they wouldn't believe you. They'd call it fantastic. The man just talks and raves incessantly... In my opinion, Earl suffers from a subconscious, deeply rooted need to be shot down, as Huey was before him.

DOCTOR. I trust you won't say that publicly...

PSYCHOLOGIST. It is no worse than some of what *he* says...

DOCTOR. So, what do we do with our problem patient? And the circus we have become embroiled in? Is he sick? Is it physical? Mental?... Political?

PSYCHOLOGIST. Then, there is only one solution. Let's send him back to Louisiana. He's their problem. I'll talk to his wife. Louisiana is probably the best answer...

DOCTOR. At least, for Texas it may be...

(Lights fade and rise on EARL and BLANCHE in the Bed Area. The "dance theme" is heard faintly. Pauses separate their speeches at first.)

BLANCHE. You seem a bit better...

EARL. I'm feeling OK...

BLANCHE. Anything you need?

EARL *(gently)*. I'd like to buy a pack of cigarettes...

BLANCHE *(turning away)*. I'm sorry, sir, but I'm a secretary, not a counter girl...

EARL. That's all right. I'm getting into politics. I need a secretary.

Act I   UNCLE EARL

BLANCHE. What's the pay?

EARL. It's not great. The hours are long. But it can be the most satisfying job I know...

BLANCHE. It sounds like work I'd like to do...

EARL. We could be a good team... *(Pause.)* I've gotten awful tired...

BLANCHE. You've been overdoing it...

EARL. I need a rest... I don't like this place much, but I know I need to get myself together... I've got a lot left to do. I got to get that loan-shark bill through...

BLANCHE. Earl...

EARL. Then, them damn segregation bills have got to be taken care of before them loony birds get us as messed up with the federal government as Faubus...

BLANCHE. Would you like...

EARL. He might be a nice man and all that, but you just don't mess around with the Feds. They got the A-bomb. Huey was the smartest man I know and even he had to know he was stepping up in class when he tried to take on the whole United States government...

BLANCHE. Are you listening to yourself? You said you need to rest. You can't go on like this. You're killing yourself. You're not God. You can't do everything.

EARL. I never said I was the Lord, but I am the governor of the state of Louisiana, and I took an oath to be governor of *all* the people. Now there are those who are trying to hurt my people and I got an obligation to keep that from happening...

BLANCHE. I have an obligation, too. I'm your wife. I can't stand by and see you kill yourself...

EARL. What's the matter, Miz Blanche? You taken to reading the *Times-Picayune*? Baton Rouge is too small for you. The pea patch ain't fancy enough. You want to go back to the high-rich-fat-silk-stocking-Mardi-Gras-to-hell-with-the-poor-society whirl? You tired of riding this old, gray nag and you want a new horse?

BLANCHE *(pause)*. I don't deserve that. And, if you were yourself, you would know I never deserved that. You're sick, Earl. I don't guess I'm helping you any by being here. *(Rises.)*

EARL *(wistfully)*. I could still use a pack of cigarettes...

BLANCHE *(not turning)*. I'm not sure the counter is open.

(She exits. EARL turns to watch her go. The "dance theme" fades. He sags. Then, turning, he roars into the night:)

EARL. Joe Arthur? Joe Arthur? Where the hell are you?

(Lights fade on him and rise severally on JOE, BILL and the ATTORNEY GENERAL as each speak. JOE is on the telephone.)

JOE. Hello, Harvey? I need to file a writ of habeas corpus in Galveston. They got Uncle Earl in some nuthouse there.

BILL. If Earl is getting out of Galveston and coming back, there are some who are gonna be glad to see him, but there are a few of us who are scared as hell as to what'll happen when he's let loose.

JOE *(still on phone)*. Uncle Earl should come free and he will.

ATTORNEY GENERAL. I can certainly testify that Uncle Earl did not go to Texas of his own free will. It took six

Act I UNCLE EARL 51

men to hold him on the stretcher on the way to the hospital.
BILL. If Earl's coming back, I suggest we get civil defense to set up evacuation routes.
JOE *(hanging up phone)*. They'll release Uncle Earl from Galveston if he'll check into Ochsner in New Orleans.
ATTORNEY GENERAL. He may check in there, but I don't know who the hell'll keep him there if he decides he doesn't want to stay.

(Lights fade on them and rise on BLANCHE and the DOCTOR.)

BLANCHE. I want to thank you for all your help, Doctor.
DOCTOR. Not at all. Are other members of the family here?
BLANCHE. I'm afraid not. I married into a highly political family...
DOCTOR. Meaning?
BLANCHE. Meaning, I suppose, that while it made family and political sense to put Earl here, it is no longer quite as clear-cut.
DOCTOR. How does it seem to you?
BLANCHE. I want what's best for Earl. And me. And everyone... What's going to happen?
DOCTOR. It seems clear that the governor intends to leave Ochsner once he gets there. I must advise you that I do not feel he is ready to be away from medical care.
BLANCHE. What are the options?
DOCTOR. Commit him to one of the state institutions. As next of kin you could have him forcibly committed to one of the state institutions from which he couldn't leave

and where the law would enable the hospital to keep him on your say.
BLANCHE. Earl won't like that.
DOCTOR. He needs help.
BLANCHE. I'm not sure I can do it.
DOCTOR. We're talking about saving his life, Miz Blanche.

(Lights fade on them and rise on "TIMES-PICAYUNE" dictating into a phone.)

"TIMES-PICAYUNE." OK. This is a phone line from Ochsner. Uncle Earl stalked out of the hospital he agreed to enter for mental and physical treatment today, and apparently set out for the capital with state troopers around him. The grim-faced governor...
JOE *(rushing in)*. What happened? Where's Uncle Earl?
"TIMES-PICAYUNE." They stopped the car, had two doctors examine him while he was still seated in the car, and had him on the way to the state hospital in Mandeville before you could blink.
JOE. They did what?
"CRAWDADDY" *(entering)*. Where's Uncle Earl?
JOE. Well, according to this fine representative of the Fourth Estate here, Uncle Earl is gone to a better place...
"CRAWDADDY." You don't mean...
JOE. No, he's not deceased, but he HAS gone to glory...
"CRAWDADDY." Joe Arthur, what ARE you talking about?
JOE *(stone-faced, but with laughter building)*. They've taken him to Southeast Hospital in Mandeville.

(JOE and the "CRAWDADDY" look at each other and begin to chuckle. Their laughter grows until they are laughing uproariously. "TIMES-PICAYUNE" stops dictating to look at them.)

JOE. I'm sure it would have been a good idea with anyone else.

"TIMES-PICAYUNE." You gone nuts?

JOE. What no one seems to have recalled is that the moment Earl set foot back in Louisiana, he was governor—with all the powers to hire and fire state officials. Mandy being a state hospital...

"TIMES-PICAYUNE" *(getting it)*. The doctors trying to hold him there against his will...

ALL. All work for *him!*

(Lights black out and rise on the Bed Area as EARL is again being wrestled into bed by the NURSE and ORDERLY. The HOSPITAL SUPERINTENDENT enters.)

EARL. Joe Arthur? Joe Arthur? Where the hell are you, Joe Arthur?

SUPERINTENDENT. Governor, I'm the superintendent of the hospital...

EARL. The hell you are. You *were* superintendent. As of now, you're unemployed.

SUPERINTENDENT. Governor, you need rest...

EARL. And you need your head examined.

SUPERINTENDENT. My mental health is not at issue.

EARL. You point your finger at me one more time you're gonna need a tool to pick your nose with.

SUPERINTENDENT. You don't seem to realize who you are and what you are.

EARL. I can tell you *exactly* who I am.

SUPERINTENDENT. And what might that be?

JOE *(enters)*. He's the man who's gonna make you the ex-superintendent as soon as he signs this paper. *(Shows document.)*

EARL *(looking at JOE ARTHUR. Slowly)*. Joe Arthur... *(Flares.)* Where the HELL you been?

BLACKOUT—END OF ACT ONE

ACT TWO

AT RISE: *In the dark, we hear a rousing political anthem. When the lights rise, we see "TIMES-PICAYUNE" phoning in another story. Perhaps there are people stringing banners and bunting around suggesting a major activity in a small town.*

"TIMES-PICAYUNE." The small southeastern Louisiana town of Covington is the focus of the state and the world today. Within hours, Uncle Earl, the governor of the state, will have his fate decided on the gym floor of the junior high school—the hearing having been moved here due to renovations to the courthouse.

The Covington Junior High School PTA is taking advantage of the windfall to set up refreshment stands, and the band and flag team are performing for the entertainment of the gathering crowd.

Entering now are some of the officials who will be participating in this drama... Yes, coming this way now is the Attorney General of the state whose job it is to represent the hospital authorities who are contesting their firing by the governor... General, General... Sir, have you any statement?

ATTORNEY GENERAL *(perspiring and clutching his briefcase)*. Yes. I want to make it crystal clear that I, in no way, oppose the governor's release from the hospital. My office will represent the hospital department and personnel and present their legal positions to the court— not in the spirit of opposing the governor's release, if warranted, but in seeing that the court has all of the law and facts at issue... Excuse me, please... *(Exits.)*

"TIMES-PICAYUNE." I think... Yes...Uncle Earl and his lawyer are making their way through the crowd, and I think the governor is going to speak...

(EARL and JOE enter amid cheers, noise, loud music and hand-waving. EARL gestures for silence.)

EARL. You all want to know why I am here today... It's very simple. I am here for the same reason that Huey is buried in front of the state Capitol... There are people who don't want you to be represented in the government of the state.

I been in three hospitals, and I'm sad to say that the one in Galveston is as far ahead of Mandy as you can throw a rock... You had to go through ten locked doors to get to me... You even had to have a key to turn on the lights... A dungeon in hell was no worse than Mandeville, and the food is as bare as the cupboard in a poor man's house... About a fifth of the people are senile, just dropped off by their kinfolks like a bag of kittens... Well, I never believed in that... When I was a kid, I picked up the kittens. People who brutalize animals are no good.

Act II UNCLE EARL 57

The superintendent there was the coldest, most contemptible man I ever saw. He threw me on the bed and I liked to have broke down and cried... I begged him not to stick that needle in me, but he tried to stick it through my pants. Then, he stuck it to the bone...

Now, as to what I did—I fired the doctors who said I was crazy, and replaced them with doctors who said I wasn't... This hearing is to determine the authorization for that... Shucks, I'm the author of authorizers... In this case, I'm like Caesar's wife—and you know she could do no harm. (I know, I know, but this is Earl.)

"CRAWDADDY" *(enters and calls).* Oyez. Oyez. Court's in session. Everyone take your places...

(Everyone moves to the Podium Area. JOE stops EARL.)

JOE. Uncle Earl, we got to settle what we been talking about...
EARL. Court's starting...
JOE. You know what's gotta happen...
EARL. We gonna be late...
JOE. This isn't my decision. I'm not telling you what to do. Miz Blanche is the one who committed you twice before. She's the only one who could commit you again. You're a lawyer. You know what step has to be taken. I'll leave the paper here. *(Puts document down.)* You do what you think has to be done.

(JOE moves to the Podium Area. EARL stands looking at the paper. The lights become mellow, autumnal. The "dance theme" is heard. EARL reads the paper. JOE

ARTHUR and the ATTORNEY GENERAL plead the case simultaneously and sotto voce. EARL's words predominate.)

EARL.	JOE.
"Suit for separation..."	Your Honor, I have several documents to file... In this, the hospital board has fired the state director of hospitals...
"...That she has publicly defamed me in committing me to Mandeville Hospital..."	
	...This fires the superintendent of Mandeville Hospital...
"She has fled the state and, therefore, my bed and board."	
	...These appoint a new state hospital director and superintendent of Mandeville Hospital. Now, I have a letter from the newly appointed superintendent...
"And has, in effect, abandoned me..."	
	It reads as follows, "I have had a lifetime acquaintance with the governor and have seen him this morning, consulted with him, and, in my opinion, there is nothing wrong with him and he should be released from this institution immediately, and I intend to do so."
"I ask for a court-supervised inventory of our community property as a prelude to the divorce..."	

JOE.
I believe the Attorney General has something to say to the court...

EARL.
"Ah, you are beautiful, my beloved,
Ah you are beautiful; your eyes are doves!"

(As the ATTORNEY GENERAL speaks, EARL signs the paper.)

ATTORNEY GENERAL.
As there is now no one with authority to hold Uncle Earl at the hospital... The State joins in a motion to discontinue...

EARL.
"You're gonna matter. You're gonna matter a lot."

Since there is no opposition to the motion, I suggest the motion be granted and the suit dismissed.

(tucking the paper in his pocket)
I can file it. It don't mean I have to do anything about it.

(All hell breaks loose. The band plays a rousing political rally song, EARL raises his arms in a victory signal, JOE and the ATTORNEY GENERAL attempt to steer EARL away. "TIMES-PICAYUNE" knifes through.)

"TIMES-PICAYUNE." What are you going to do now, Earl?

EARL. I'm gonna be governor. *(JOE and the ATTORNEY GENERAL work him toward the bed.)* If you got any tips on the ponies, keep them for a few days.

"TIMES-PICAYUNE." Will you follow the advice of your doctors?

EARL. My intention is to do what my doctors say. But, if I think they might be erroneous, I'd reserve my rights to do otherwise.

(JOE, the ATTORNEY GENERAL, "CRAWDADDY," LUCILLE and, perhaps, others, cluster around EARL as he gets in bed.)

EARL. I have never been insane one second in my life. I love Louisiana; I love its people, its institutions, its schools... Through its fine people, I have been honored many times. I would never let those fine people down. *(Looks for LUCILLE.)* Lucille, I'm hungry.

LUCILLE. And when aren't you? *(To "CRAWDADDY.")* There's a plate in the kitchenette. *("CRAWDADDY" leaves.)*

EARL. I am grateful to everyone who helped me gain my freedom. I especially appreciate the prayers that were said for me by the Catholics, Baptists, Methodists, the Church of God, and, in fact, by those of all faiths.

"TIMES-PICAYUNE" *(to JOE)*. Good God, he's going to run again. *(JOE nods.)*

EARL. As I have stated on many occasions, I am a good friend of the poor white man, the poor colored man, as well as those among the rich who want to do right.

LUCILLE. Here's your plate, Earl. Eat every bite.

EARL. From the bottom of my heart, I want to thank everyone for their thoughtfulness, for the help they have given me, and, again, above all, for their prayers.

(LUCILLE hands him a plate of food. As he eats, she begins to recite.)

LUCILLE. Let us rejoice that, once again, Right has overcome...
"Out of the night that covers me,
Black as the Pit from pole to pole,
I thank whatever gods may be
For my unconquerable soul..."

EARL. ...Unconquerable and indestructible soul...
LUCILLE.
"In the fell clutch of Circumstance
I have not winced nor cried aloud.
Under the bludgeonings of Chance,
My head is Bloody, but Unbowed..."

(Fade out as she continues the poem. In the dark we hear the VOICE of AUNTIE ALICE calling:)

ALICE. Li'l Earl? Li'l Earl? Come on home, boy.

(The lights rise on her as she stands as before. She looks off in the distance and speaks yearningly:)

Li'l Earl? You come when your Auntie Alice calls. Where are you, Li'l Earl? Is you lost? Where are you?

(The lights fade on her as we hear "Foggy Mountain Breakdown" which will run through the following segments, separating and punctuating each incident. When the lights come up we see a flushed EARL sitting on the bed in his BVDs, dictating a press release over the telephone. There is about him the air of a small boy on holiday having an absolutely marvelous time.)

EARL. Hello? Hello? You there? All right, here's the statement you wanted, and I hope it satisfies you. "I want to apologize for the episode in the elevator last night... But that man *did* try to force his way in where he wasn't wanted. But, I'll forget it and I hope he can..." What do you mean?... No, I damn well *won't* pay for his tetanus shot... If he hadn't stuck his finger in my face, I wouldn't have bit it...

(Music rises and builds as the lights black out. Across the stage, lights rise on JOE on the phone.)

JOE. Now, to one can of cream of chicken soup, add three-quarters of a can of cold water... That's right... Bring to a boil and simmer slowly... Yep... Now, while the soup is simmering, add two cans of diced Vi-enna sausage and fold it into the soup until the meat is warmed through... Then you serve it with iced water and crackers... Yes, I'm sure that's the way Uncle Earl cooked it in his hotel room... Can you call it "Uncle Earl Soup" on your café menu?... Well, I'm sure he won't mind... What? Yep, Uncle Earl sure knows his soup... Goodbye...

Act II UNCLE EARL 63

(Slams phone down. Music up and lights out. Lights on EARL on phone.)

EARL. Reporters and photographers have been chasing me like a wild animal. And they could drive me insane. I'm human, and I make a lot of mistakes. If the press keeps after me as it has, then the only way I can stay alive is to escape from the press.

(Music up and lights out. Lights on JOE on phone.)

JOE. It is NOT true that the governor entered the First Baptist Church of El Paso wearing a hat and smoking a cigarette... It IS true that, by way of compliment, he told the minister on his way out, "That was good preaching. It was only thirty-five minutes long. In the country, they preach for an hour and a half..." *(Groans.)* Yes, he DID add, "That's too long for an old man to sleep..."

(Music up and lights out. Lights on EARL on phone.)

EARL. I was getting along FINE in Louisiana. And, I hasten to apologize for any mistakes I made in Texas. I probably got nutty and said some things I shouldn't have. As for my remarks at the airport about getting a pistol, that shows how a man can get whipped up—

(Music up and lights out. Lights on JOE on phone.)

JOE. Of COURSE the governor is all right... *(Sighs.)* No, he normally does NOT take his dentures out in public restaurants... He was trying to eat a peaceful meal when he saw some photographers trying to snap some shots of him, and it was his way of trying to discourage them... We are sorry if the other diners were inconvenienced—particularly the lady with what I believe is called a "low gag reflex."

(Music up and lights out. Lights on EARL on phone.)

EARL. I don't want to hurt anyone. I don't know any newspaper people I have tried to hurt. But, I'm not going to lose my life because of continued harassment. I'm a peaceful man and I'm liable to hurt someone if they don't let me alone. They're not running or bluffing old Earl anymore...

(Music up and lights out. Lights on JOE on phone.)

JOE *(elaborate sigh)*. The governor does NOT normally eat with a brown paper bag over his head... Is there any way to convince you people that there are times when Uncle Earl simply does not want to have his picture taken?... I KNOW what the sight of pompano disappearing into a mouth hole in a brown paper bag is like... I was at the table with him... What lady? She did what?... Again? Say, you don't suppose the same one is following us around, do you?

(Music up and lights out. Lights on EARL on phone.)

EARL. I just made up my mind I didn't want any pictures taken of me, so I held them off as much as my condition would permit... Of course I cut a breathing hole in the pillowcase. You wouldn't want me to suffocate, would you?... Sure I'll pay for the pillowcase... Goodbye. *(Hangs up and calls.)* Joe Arthur, I think I'm getting tired of Texas. Let's head West. *(Grumbles.)* A hell of a vacation this is turning out to be.

(Music up and lights out. Lights on JOE on phone.)

JOE. This man is the governor of the state of Louisiana; he is a mature man and he is potty trained. He did *not* urinate in your hall... He DID say something about the flowers on your wallpaper needing watering... *(Trails off.)* What?... Well, we were planning to head West... *(Questioning.)* Alert your other branches?... *(Stiffly.)* Well, sir, if you feel the need, THAT is up to you. *(Slams down phone with offended dignity. Hesitates, thinking. Starts off, calling:)* Uncle Earl, could I ask you something about last night...?

(Music up and lights out. Lights on EARL at the Podium. "CRAWDADDY" stands to one side. "TIMES-PICAYUNE" is joined by a SECOND REPORTER. A PHOTOGRAPHER is also in evidence. JOE is on the other side of EARL. A press conference is going on.)

EARL. Now, I don't need any doctors. I can diagnose my own case better than anybody in the world and I never had no stroke, despite what those crack-proof doctors said.

"TIMES-PICAYUNE." Governor, have you any comment on the impeachment resolution that is supposedly going to be introduced at the special session of the legislature?

EARL. The man who introduces it will end up lighter and wiser... I know the legislature is upset with me. When I talked to them last, I stepped on the toes of sleeping cats, but I will happily meet and talk to any legislator—though some of the things I say to them might scorch their undershorts.

SECOND REPORTER. Governor, we understand you might be invited to address the Texas state legislature. Any observations on the oil industry in this state compared to your own?

EARL. You have a number of mighty good oilmen in this state who contribute heavily to the welfare of the state. But, you also have some who wouldn't pay a dime to see Christ rescued from the cross.

"TIMES-PICAYUNE." The IRS is investigating you.

EARL. They've done it before and found nothing. They'll never find a thing.

SECOND REPORTER. One of their areas of investigation has to do with your gambling winnings.

EARL. They want to tax that?

"TIMES-PICAYUNE." Yes, sir.

EARL. It never dawned on me you'd owe income tax on gambling money, because, all my life, my losses were greater than my gains. And that's true with the average American who is sucker enough to try to beat the horses and bingo and the lottery and the slots. Lotteries and the slot machines are two of the lousiest ways to gamble there are. Makes me mad just to look at the slots.

"TIMES-PICAYUNE." What's your favorite kind of gambling, Uncle Earl?

EARL. Horses. My old grandfather got run out of Mississippi for racing horses on a Sunday. He come over here

Act II UNCLE EARL 67

to hunt, race horses and to fish. I like horseracing and I make no bones about it. That's why I don't believe the *Times-Picayune* is sincere about stopping gambling. The biggest temptation to a would-be gambler is the pari-mutuel betting results they publish.

JOE. Uh, Uncle Earl...

SECOND REPORTER. About your trouble with the press... You've filed a libel suit against *Time-Life*. Any comment?

EARL. Mr. Luce, the publisher, is like a man that owns a shoe store and buys all the shoes to fit himself. Then he expects other people to buy them. They just overstepped. And I called them on it.

SECOND REPORTER. Where do you think you've won the most gambling?

EARL. Betting on my campaigns.

JOE. Uhhhh, Uncle Earl...

SECOND REPORTER. Betting on your campaigns?

EARL. It's always possible to place a wager on the outcome of a campaign—especially in Louisiana. As far as campaigns go, I'm a super-duper...

JOE *(nervous)*. Uh, Uncle Earl, we got to be getting on...

EARL. I hope to take some money in the coming campaign from those who are able to lose it.

JOE *(more so)*. Thanks for coming, folks...

EARL. I won't take any money from anybody who has less than a million dollars. With that kind of money, I should be able to use it like I want to.

JOE *(really nervous)*. We've got to go...

EARL. Of course, I'll have a big set-to with the federal government after I win it...

JOE *(desperate)*. That's it! This press conference is over. Goodbye.

(He shoos out the SECOND REPORTER and the PHOTOGRAPHER. "TIMES-PICAYUNE" is able to circle back to EARL.)

"TIMES-PICAYUNE" *(furtively)*. Uncle Earl! Uncle Earl!
EARL. What's the matter with you?
"TIMES-PICAYUNE." You dropped your wallet at the pari-mutuel window.
EARL. Oh. *(Takes wallet.)* Thanks a lot.
"TIMES-PICAYUNE." Aren't you going to count it. There's $1500 in there.
EARL. I trust you. You're a reporter, not a publisher.
"TIMES-PICAYUNE." How much did you win today?
EARL. Oh. $100 or so.
"TIMES-PICAYUNE." You don't seem very pleased about it.
EARL. Not my money. Campaign money.
"TIMES-PICAYUNE." You're gambling with campaign money?
EARL. It WAS given to me to use as I see fit. Got to build a war chest. You got any idea how tight money gets in a second primary when the losers start ganging up on the leader?
"TIMES-PICAYUNE." Where you going now, Uncle Earl?
EARL. Shopping. I want to buy some clothes for the poor white folks and the poor colored folks up by my pea patch.

Act II UNCLE EARL

(Music rises and lights change. Rise on HOTEL CLERK. JOE enters.)

CLERK. May I help you, sir?
JOE. I hope I'm at the right hotel?
CLERK. Whom do you wish to locate, sir?
JOE *(checking watch)*. I'm to meet the governor of Louisiana and his party here. Have they...?
CLERK. He hasn't registered, but he has reservations.
JOE. He's late...
CLERK *(looks around conspiratorially)*. Not to worry, sir. We're following him by radio. He just went through Colorado Springs at 100 miles an hour.

(Sound of SIREN fills the room. JOE clutches his head as the lights fade and music builds. Rise on Farm Area. EARL is sitting on an overturned grocery cart covered with brown bags, bread, cold cuts and condiments. He is talking to "TIMES-PICAYUNE.")

EARL. After I eat... Fix yourself a sandwich... I want to go to some hardware stores and some leather stores and some saddle stores. You know I'm a bargain hunter... They say if you buy something you don't need, it's no bargain, no matter what you paid for it, but I can't quite see that.
"TIMES-PICAYUNE." What about that $900 worth of boots you bought in Fort Worth?
EARL. I didn't buy but $287 worth. I'm not going to tell you he gave them to me at half price... He wanted to give them to me outright and I wouldn't have them... Marshall Field in Chicago or a little store in north Loui-

siana is just the same. They'll all take a little less if you hold out... Want another sandwich?

"TIMES-PICAYUNE." I'm fine, Uncle Earl.

EARL. You know, I'm enjoying this. All that fancy stuff you get in restaurants gives me stomach trouble.

(There is noise offstage. "CRAWDADDY" enters, feebly remonstrating with an OLD LADY.)

EARL. What's the matter?

"CRAWDADDY." I'm sorry, Uncle Earl. I been trying to keep her away, but she won't stay put.

EARL. What's the matter, ma'am?

OLD LADY. This officer wouldn't let me come near you.

EARL. Well, he's a little overprotective sometimes...

"CRAWDADDY." She's talking crazy...

EARL. Well, she's in good company. Let her come on, Crawdaddy...

OLD LADY. I just wanted to get near you.

EARL. You from Louisiana?

OLD LADY. No, no. I've lived all my life here in New Mexico.

EARL. Is there anything I can do for you in Louisiana?

OLD LADY. No. I don't even know anyone there.

EARL. Well, why'd you want to see me?

OLD LADY. I didn't.

EARL. Then, why were you fighting with the officer?

OLD LADY. Oh. Well... I've been reading about you in the newspapers...

EARL. Who hasn't?

OLD LADY. And I just wanted to get close enough to hear you cuss.

Act II UNCLE EARL 71

EARL. To hear me cuss?
OLD LADY. Umm-hummm...
EARL. Well, I'll be a yellow-tailed son of a bitch.
OLD LADY. Oooooh! Thank you!!

(Blackout. Lights rise on JOE and the SECOND RE-PORTER.)

JOE. I have a short release as regards the forty-five-minute meeting between the governor of Louisiana and former President Truman. The governor requested the meeting because, and I quote: "I want to talk to Harry about possible Democratic candidates for president next year. I'm foolish enough to think I'll be re-elected and have something to do with the Louisiana delegation to the National Convention," Unquote.
SECOND REPORTER. Anything on the substance of the conversation?
JOE. They discussed possible candidates. The governor said he thought Senator Kennedy too young to be president and that "he looked even younger than he is." He also told President Truman a number of dirty jokes.
SECOND REPORTER. Any personal observations?
JOE. Yes. It may be the first time in his life former President Truman was unable to get in a word of conversation.
SECOND REPORTER. Where does the governor go from here?
JOE. I believe he's returning to Louisiana to run for re-election as governor.

(Blackout. In the dark, we hear a bluesy Sophie Tucker song. Lights rise on the Podium where EARL is in customary attire and attitude for campaigning.)

EARL. Let me introduce myself... I am "Crazy Old Earl," governor of the state of Louisiana... They say I'm crazy... They say that I'm a wild animal... I will let you decide here today whether or not I'm a wild animal...

When I got off that plane in Texas, I felt like a muley bull coming out of a dipping vat. They snatched me out without even enough clothes on me to cover a red bug. A week after I arrived in Texas, I was enjoying the same wardrobe. I used to have crazy people coming in my room all night. One of them thought my room was the toilet.

The *Times-Picayune* is trying to tell you how to vote. Don't let *no* rascal buy your vote or tell you who to vote for. If you believe them, I've got a pistol in each pocket, and a blackjack in each hand, and you'd believe I grab senators by the neck and legislators by the tail.

THIS is the same newspaper that wants you to vote for the Hillbilly Singer. He's in Shreveport on Sunday morning singing "Nearer My God to Thee" and in Donaldsonville that night singing "Bed Bug Blues."

He loves money like a hog loves slop. You couldn't wake him up with an earthquake. He won't say nothing. He won't promise nothing, and, if he gets in, he won't *do* nothing.

Act II UNCLE EARL 73

(Fade to black. In the dark, we hear a telephone RING. The "dance theme" builds as the lights rise to reveal EARL and BLANCHE on phones on opposite sides of the stage.)

EARL. Hello.
BLANCHE. Hello.
EARL. I've missed you.
BLANCHE. I've missed you.
EARL. I heard you'd gone to Colorado.
BLANCHE. I thought it best. I heard what you said you'd do to me.
EARL. Now, you can't believe the damn newspapers...
BLANCHE. It was my sister. You called her.
EARL. Yeah, well, that... I got a little angry with her... You know how I feel, Miz Blanche...
BLANCHE. I'm afraid I do...
EARL. It's just that... You don't know what it's like to be locked up. How could you do that to me? I couldn't do it to you. I couldn't do it to anybody... I couldn't destroy a person's humanness that way...
BLANCHE. I was trying to save your life.
EARL. You were just damn hateful-jealous about some lying newspaper story about me and some woman. How the hell could anybody believe the *Times-Picayune*? If they reported the Second Coming of Christ, they'd get His Name wrong.
BLANCHE. I don't care about any stories...
EARL. There hasn't been any decent, nice-looking woman employed by me that you didn't worry about. How can an old man like me take care of three or four women, when I'd do well to take care of you, and know I'm do-

ing a bum job at that! That's why you tried to get rid of me—not that I blame you...

BLANCHE. Why do you do this? Night after night...

EARL. Don't start, dammit. Don't start. You make it out to be my fault, when all I'm asking is that you come back to me. I'll do anything. I'll pay any price. Just come back to me.

BLANCHE. The price is simple. Get out of politics. It's killing you. I don't want you dead. *(EARL says nothing. There is a long pause.)* Earl? Earl...

(She waits then slowly hangs up. Lights fade on BLANCHE. EARL stands holding the receiver as LUCILLE enters with a plate of food.)

LUCILLE. You on the phone?

EARL *(hanging up)*. No... I'm not talking to anyone.

LUCILLE. I brought you some food.

EARL. Thank you.

LUCILLE. Sit down and eat. *(He does, listlessly. She hesitates.)* Earl? You ever think of calling Blanche? Just to talk?

EARL *(eating)*. She's all right; we just can't get along. It's better for us to be apart before we shoot each other or something... *(Braggadocio.)* Why, if I weren't in politics, I would have divorced her long ago.

LUCILLE. I worry about you... I worry about her. You're two people made to be together...

EARL. You don't have to worry about Miz Blanche. She got the money all right. She got plenty to take care of herself, and she has plenty left over to take care of Uncle Earl, if she wants to.

LUCILLE. Blanche didn't care about your money, Earl...

EARL. She took me for a couple hundred thousand when she filed her own divorce suit. Not that I'm in trouble. I had a long-shot wildcat oil well come in and dropped $300,000 on me—enough for me to live like a gentleman at the pea patch among my friends and neighbors, both white and colored, for three lifetimes...

LUCILLE. You're getting excited. Just try to eat...

EARL. I'm not hungry now. I feel like calling Miz Blanche and cussing her out.

LUCILLE. Oh, Earl, please don't...

EARL. 'Course, I don't know where she is, so I'll just call one of her sisters and give her the same medicine.

LUCILLE. You'll only make things worse...

EARL *(picks up phone and dials)*. Hello?... Well, who the hell does it sound like?... I don't know where your sister is, so I've got a few things to tell you, you broom-flying witch...

(LUCILLE takes plate off, crying. EARL stands for a moment and slowly hangs up the phone. Lights become mellow. After a moment, "CRAWDADDY" enters.)

"CRAWDADDY." Evening, Uncle Earl.

EARL. Evening, Crawdaddy...

"CRAWDADDY." Quiet night...

EARL. Depends on what the day's been like...

"CRAWDADDY." I guess that's the truth...

EARL. How'd you spend your day?

"CRAWDADDY." Did a little yard work. Played with my kids...

EARL. Yeah. Them's some fine kids you got...

"CRAWDADDY." I like 'em...

EARL. I been thinking...

"CRAWDADDY." Yes, Uncle Earl?

EARL. For all the good it ever did me... I don't know... Like, if it wasn't for the colored people down here, me and Huey wouldn't have had a chance in politics...

"CRAWDADDY." A lot of people wouldn't...

EARL. Me and my brother done more for the colored than anybody in the whole South. It's a shame how they been treated, and we're just going to have to realize, sooner or later, that they just like anybody else; that they've got a soul, and they'll go to heaven, and, sooner or later, we're going to have to live with them... Of course, if I said that publicly, I wouldn't get a vote among the white people.

"CRAWDADDY." Not these days...

EARL. Right now, a nigra ain't got hardly a chance in this state. They can challenge his right to vote and prevent him from being registered... But, you just wait and see what I'm going to do in this coming special session of the legislature. I'm going to pass a state law that's going to make it easier for them to vote. But, I'm going to have a hell of a lot of opposition...

"CRAWDADDY." I'm sure you'll do whatever you think right, Uncle Earl... You got all the time there is... I just *know* your ticket is going to win.

EARL *(looks at him affectionately. Pats his arm. Turns front and stares off into space. Quietly).* They are going to beat the living HELL out of us...

(Lights fade on "CRAWDADDY's" stricken look. In the dark, there is a raucous blast of strip music. Lights come

Act II   UNCLE EARL   77

up dimly on FANNY in full gyrations and small costume. As she gets into her act, EARL, JOE and "CRAW-DADDY" enter on the periphery of the scene.)

JOE. Governor, Governor, we've got to go back.
EARL. I wanna see some strip shows.
"CRAWDADDY." You shouldn't have let Uncle Earl drive.
JOE. I thought he knew what a one-way street was.
"CRAWDADDY." That city cop is some mad...
EARL. Let's get over to Bourbon Street. The shows are on.
JOE. That policeman wanted your driver's license. You showed him a hunting license.
EARL. Hell, Joe Arthur, what you think I'm doing in the French Quarter?... Let's try over there.
"CRAWDADDY." Is this a good idea?
JOE. Only if you're a kamikaze pilot...

(Strip music blares and lights build on the nightclub set as FANNY reaches the end of her act. EARL, JOE and "CRAWDADDY" go to a table. EARL stands and applauds at the end of the dance, waving JOE and "CRAWDADDY" to their feet.)

EARL. Tell that little lady I'd like her to have a drink with me.
"CRAWDADDY." Governor, I've got to warn you, I hear she's got a very mean husband...
EARL. Hell, I only want to talk with her. I know I'm supposed to be crazy, but you don't think I'm gonna mount her on the dance floor, do you?
JOE. Do we all get a vote?

EARL. ...All right. Tell her to bring a friend. *("CRAW-DADDY" exits.)*
JOE. Governor, is this really a good idea?
EARL. Joe Arthur, you worry too much. I done lost the election; I'm on my way out of office; my wife isn't speaking to me; and the IRS is examining me closer than a proctologist ever could. Now, how much more trouble could I get into?
JOE. We'll probably find out... Here come the girls.

("CRAWDADDY" enters with FANNY and BOOTY who have coats over their outfits. Though overly made up, they are not tramps.)

"CRAWDADDY." Governor, these young ladies want to meet you. This is Fanny and Booty.
JOE. You have got to be kidding me...
EARL. Which is which?
BOOTY. I'm Booty. It's my stage name.
JOE. I don't want to know why.
BOOTY. I wear chaps and spurs.
JOE. I had to ask.
"CRAWDADDY." Is Fanny your stage name, too?
FANNY. As a matter of fact it was my grandmother's name.
EARL. Shame on you, Crawdaddy...
"CRAWDADDY." I didn't mean nothing...
EARL. Ladies, won't you have a seat?
FANNY. Governor... Gentlemen...
BOOTY. So nice to see you...
EARL. Can I get you anything to drink? Or eat?
FANNY. They don't serve food here.

JOE. I wouldn't eat it if they did...
EARL. What's that, Joe Arthur?
JOE. Nothing, Uncle Earl.
BOOTY. What about tamales? I love tamales.
EARL. Then we are soul mates, 'cause I do, too. *(Tosses bill to "CRAWDADDY.")* Get us a mess of tamales. *("CRAWDADDY" exits.)* I just loved your act.
FANNY. Thank you very much. I don't meet many governors.
EARL. That's funny. I've met nearly every stripper on Bourbon Street the last few months.
BOOTY. So we heard...
EARL. Well, tell me, you like stripping?
BOOTY. It's an art form.
FANNY. I like it. My husband Bruno isn't crazy about the idea. Especially at the moment...
EARL. Why do you say that?
FANNY. Because he's heading this way and he's got a gun.
JOE. 'Scuse me, miss, but would you like to examine the floor?

(JOE and BOOTY slide under the table as BRUNO nears the foursome. He is armed, irate and rather drunk.)

BRUNO. What you do?
EARL. What's he say?
FANNY. "What you do?"
EARL. Oh. Foreign?
FANNY. The gun's American.
EARL. 'Scuse me there, podner. You got a problem?
BRUNO. You make my wife, I kill you.

EARL. You give an old man a lot of credit… Could we talk about this?

BRUNO. I kill…

EARL. Yeah, well, Smith and Wesson makes more than one of those, you know… *(EARL draws a gun of his own.)* You pretty good with that thing?

BRUNO *(waving gun)*. You want find out?

EARL. Well, within reason… You think you can shoot out those stage lights?

BRUNO. Can you?

EARL. Well, hell, let's see… *(They take turns shooting at the stage lights and breaking them until EARL misses.)* Well, you were right. You're the better shot. How about a drink?

BRUNO. I drink.

EARL. I hope the hell you pass out, too. Barkeep? Triples! *(To FANNY.)* He do this a lot?

FANNY *(shaken)*. Yes…

EARL. Why'd you marry him?

FANNY. I work on Bourbon Street and I'm alone.

EARL. You wanted protection…

FANNY. Everyone wants to be cared for, don't they?

EARL *(after a pause)*. You like bread pudding?

FANNY. I guess so. Why?

EARL. Let's go have some.

FANNY. Where?

EARL. The Mansion.

FANNY. In Baton Rouge?

EARL. 'Less they moved it to get me out.

FANNY *(pointing to BRUNO)*. What about him?

EARL. If he likes bread pudding, bring him, too. *(Leans under the table.)* Joe Arthur, you coming?

JOE *(emerging with BOOTY)*. Yes, Uncle Earl.
"CRAWDADDY" *(entering)*. Here's the tamales.
EARL. Bring 'em along. We're going to get dessert ready.

(Music builds as JOE and "CRAWDADDY" carry BRUNO offstage. The lights change to reveal EARL and FANNY at the Mansion.)

FANNY. I hear tell you and your missus don't see eye-to-eye.
EARL. You have a rare gift for understatement.
FANNY. What's that mean?
EARL. It means you're right. She's a fine woman, but let her go her way, and I'll go mine. I think we both better off that way.
FANNY. You like her?
EARL. You like yours? *(Phone rings.)* Answer that.
FANNY *(answers phone)*. Hello. *(To EARL.)* I think it's a drunk. He wants to talk to "Ol' Squirrelly," he says.
EARL. Tell him I went to Africa with a load of lizards. *(She hesitates.)* Just hang up. *(She does.)* Happens all the time. You get used to it...
FANNY. How'd you get into this mess?
EARL. Just being myself.
FANNY. And, who's that?
EARL. Somebody who did right as he saw it.
FANNY. Oh, I see. You some kind of do-gooder?
EARL. I'm a politician. A politician is misunderstood. He is capable of doing something for the people. That's what I tried to do.
FANNY. And all THIS happened?

EARL. All this... You know, I don't know that it would have all gone this far without them pin-headed nuts and their segregation bills...

(Lights change, isolating EARL in a limbo, removed from time and space, as he muses, evaluating himself.)

I suppose I was too old... I just couldn't go along on this one... Maybe I pushed myself too far, too hard, like Miz Blanche says, but those skinheads were going to hurt a lot of colored people and a lot of good white people with a lot of laws that probably went against the Constitution to begin with... And for what? In twenty years when all this Integration-Segregation stuff is over, what you gonna be left with?... You still gonna have the "haves" and the "have-nots"...and the "have-nots" are still gonna need help and the "haves" ain't gonna want to give it to them...so, somebody like Huey or me will still be needed.

They killed Huey. They tried to put me in the nuthouse and throw the key away... And for what?...because we couldn't keep our mouths shut when we saw something wrong. If I gotta go, I can't think of a better way than to be swinging at some fat cat with his hand in some poor man's pockets... *(Phone rings. Lights return to previous setting.)* Answer that, will you.

FANNY. Hello?... It sounds like a student. A kid.

EARL. Gimme that. *(Takes the phone from her. Covers it.)* They play a joke on the freshmen at LSU. They give them this number to call for a message so they'll get embarrassed when they hear, "Governor's Mansion."

Act II   UNCLE EARL   83

(Into phone.) Hello? This is Uncle Earl. I just wanted to call out there to see how you doing, 'cause I know your daddy. He's a fine man, and I want you to know that if there's anything I can ever do for you, all you have to do is call... You welcome... G'night... *(Hangs up.)*
FANNY. Who was that?
EARL. Haven't the faintest idea... But he'll always know he talked to the governor...and that he gave a damn.
FANNY. I don't know if everybody would, but I think *you* do...

(JOE, "CRAWDADDY" and BOOTY enter.)

JOE. Uncle Earl, we got to be thinking about clearing out. Your term's up in a couple of days. We gotta pack. We ought to get the girls home.
EARL. You right. Thank you for your company, ladies...
BOOTY. This is so sad...
JOE. "Que sera..."
FANNY. Wait. What about one last strip for the governor? Play some music.

(FANNY and BOOTY take off their coats to reveal their costumes. "CRAWDADDY" turns up the radio to a rock song. The GIRLS dance to it, a spirited, anarchic coda to Earl's term of office. The MEN clap to the rhythm of the song. The mood is bright and happy.)

JOE. It's gonna be hard to leave this, ain't it, Uncle Earl?
EARL *(enjoying himself)*. What?... Yeah... Joe Arthur?
JOE. Yes, Uncle Earl?

EARL. Did you know that the congressional seat in the Eighth District is up for grabs? *(JOE wheels to face him.)* Whatd'ya say, Joe Arthur? One more time?

(JOE ARTHUR throws his hands up. Music and dance build. Blackout. When the lights rise, EARL is at the Podium, delivering his last campaign speech. It is a hot night. The Coke and hanky are in use as at the beginning of the play. He swabs at strategic points in his speech.)

EARL. I'm not against anybody for reasons of race, creed, or any "ism" he might believe in, except for nuttism, skin-game-ism, or communism...

I'm glad to see so many of my fine, Catholic friends here—they been so kind to me I sometimes say I consider myself forty percent Catholic and sixty percent Baptist. But, I'm in favor of *every* religion—with the possible exception of snake-chunking... Anybody who so presumes on how he stands with Providence that he will let a snake bite him, I say he deserves what he's got coming to him...

Now, this sapsucker who's running against me thinks he's gonna cause me a lot of trouble with you... Oh, yeah!... He's been telling you the horrible secret that Uncle Earl been seen in the company of stripteasers... Now, what has that got to do with running for Congress?

And, anyhow, I'm not a married man. I can go out with a pretty girl if I want to. Besides, let's think a minute.

I'm sixty-four years old; I've just had prostate surgery; I've been locked up in the nuthouse; I've had a heart attack; I've lost over thirty pounds—look at me in this collar... *(Shows looseness.)* now, I ask you... If I'm chasing girls, what do you think I could do with one if I caught her?

And this from a man who was born with a silver spoon in his mouth that he couldn't get out with a crowbar! He's the only man I know can talk out of the both sides of his mouth and whistle at the same time. *(Surveys crowd.)* Now this is what I like to see—everybody standing together. Not all our colored friends in one spot and our white friends in another. I'm the best friend the poor white man, and the middle-class white man, and the rich white man (so long as he behaves himself), and the poor colored man ever had in the state of Louisiana... And if the NAACP, and those pin-headed nuts who want to re-fight the Civil War will just leave us alone, then sensible people, not cranks, can get along in a reasonable way...

Now, I got a few hams and watermelons I want to give out to you good people. Ain't no bribe. Just a gift from somebody who's known what it is to be hungry, and who thinks it's better to give than receive... This here first ham is going to go to the biggest, blackest, ugliest nigra in the crowd. You know who you are, so come on up and get it.

(Lights fade on EARL and find "TIMES-PICAYUNE" in a panic. JOE and "CRAWDADDY" call to him.)

"CRAWDADDY." Hey, Times-Picayune, where you going?

JOE. Times-Picayune thought there'd be an explosion...

"TIMES-PICAYUNE." I thought to myself, this is it. He's gone too far.

JOE. That so?

"TIMES-PICAYUNE." You got these Freedom Riders all over the South. You got this Reverend King in Alabama... And HE offers a ham to the ugliest...

JOE. Sure did...

"TIMES-PICAYUNE." He IS crazy, I thought. How's he think he can get away with this?

"CRAWDADDY." What did Uncle Earl do?

"TIMES-PICAYUNE." He pointed and said, "You! Yeah, you!... You're the blackest and ugliest."

(EARL's VOICE picks up the line.)

EARL *(off)*. You're the blackest and ugliest. Come on up here and get this ham.

"CRAWDADDY." So what did the man do?

"TIMES-PICAYUNE." He came up and got the ham! *(JOE and "CRAWDADDY" laugh.)* I just don't understand...

JOE. It's not really that hard. Earl and his family have done a lot of living here: a lot of politicking; a lot of doing for people; a lot of loving.

"CRAWDADDY." People don't forget.

JOE. People don't forget that, when you come down to it, all you got's each other. It's a cold world otherwise...

(Their LAUGHTER builds and is joined by LAUGHTER that echoes from all sides of the auditorium, building to

Act II UNCLE EARL 87

a peak as the lights fade, and resolving to the sound of one offstage LAUGH as the lights rise on BLANCHE in the Farm Area.)

EARL. I'm sorry, Miz Blanche. I haven't been home for a while and I just had to talk to that old rascal for a minute.
BLANCHE. I'm all right.
EARL. I like the old devil.
BLANCHE. You like everybody.
EARL. I suppose. Human beings are the most interesting things in the world. And I love to hear people talk about themselves, especially if it's somebody I like. It helps me to understand them.
BLANCHE. Let's sit a minute.
EARL *(dusts log)*. Let me... The pea patch ain't the cleanest place in the world...
BLANCHE. But it's home...
EARL. Yeah... Not that our place in Baton Rouge wasn't nice...
BLANCHE. I know... That refrigerator in the kitchen...
EARL. What about it?
BLANCHE. Was that ours?
EARL. Still is.
BLANCHE. That's the refrigerator I tried to give away.
EARL. It was our first refrigerator.
BLANCHE. It was twenty-four years old when I tried to give it away.
EARL. Well, I wanted to keep it.
BLANCHE. Why?
EARL. It was our first refrigerator... Your friend liked the one you ended up donating...

BLANCHE. Should have. It was brand new.

EARL *(pause)*. You going to vote in the election?

BLANCHE. Always do. It'd be a sorry thing if the Democratic National Committeewoman didn't.

EARL. Who you gonna vote for?

BLANCHE. The best man...

EARL *(after a pause)*. Dinner good?

BLANCHE. Delicious.

EARL. Sadie sure can cook... You still look the same as ever... *(Car horn blows.)*

BLANCHE. My sister. It must be time to go.

EARL. I'll help to pack the car. There's some good turnip greens I want you to take back with you. *(They look at each other for a moment. EARL exits. The "dance theme" builds. BLANCHE looks after him.)*

BLANCHE. You have mattered... And, together, I suppose we have mattered about as much as any two people can... I wish we'd had more time... I wish...

(Music rises as she stands, thinking her own thoughts, and the lights fade. She slowly exits as they do. In the dark we hear a rustle of VOICES. When the lights rise, we see JOE and "CRAWDADDY" putting an obviously ill EARL in bed.)

JOE. Get his other leg. OK, now, swing him easy into the bed. Easy. Easy!... Lay him down.

"CRAWDADDY." Joe Arthur, he needs a doctor. He needs a doctor bad.

EARL. No doctor.

JOE. No doctor, Uncle Earl...

"CRAWDADDY." You're sick, Uncle Earl. Bad sick. You ought to be in the hospital.

EARL. If I go in the hospital now, I'll lose a lot of votes from people who figure I'll die. I'd rather stay in this hotel room, win the election, and then die...than go to the hospital, lose the election, and live.

"CRAWDADDY." But, Uncle Earl...

EARL. Dammit, the polls is open. People are voting right now. You couldn't keep it quiet.

JOE. What do you want to do, Uncle Earl?

EARL. I think I ate something that disagreed with me...

JOE. A case of ptomaine poisoning... I'll see to it... *(Exits.)*

"CRAWDADDY." Why don't you get some rest, Governor?

EARL. I got a long time to rest... *(Drifts off.)* If I could beat him, I'd die happy...

(Lights dim on EARL in the bed. "CRAWDADDY" leaves. The lights build on the Farm Area. AUNTIE ALICE enters with a load of wash. She is humming "In the Garden." After a few moments, we hear:)

LITTLE EARL *(offstage)*. Auntie Alice. Auntie Alice! *(Enters.)*

ALICE. What's the matter with you, Little Earl?

LITTLE EARL. Paw butchered some hogs and he gave me the insides.

ALICE. You selling them down by the colored shacks again?

LITTLE EARL. Fifteen cents a tub.

ALICE. I'll have to buy me some. They's good, if you know how to fix 'em.
LITTLE EARL. You don't have to buy them. *(Kisses her on the cheek.)* I saved a tub to give you.
ALICE *(disengaging gently)*. Lord, honey, don't do that. Suppose some white folks come by and see you?
LITTLE EARL. Why would that matter?
ALICE. Folks wouldn't like it.
LITTLE EARL. Don't you love me?
ALICE. That's got nothing to do with it.
LITTLE EARL. Mama says God says we supposed to love each other.
ALICE. God don't live in Louisiana. I got to.
LITTLE EARL. Then you don't love God...
ALICE. I'm just telling you the way the world is.
LITTLE EARL. Then he world is wrong, 'cause I know my mama and God is right.
ALICE *(embracing him)*. Oh, honey, come on home... Come home...

(Lights dim on the Farm Area. JOE enters the dimly lit bedroom. The lights brighten on it.)

JOE. Uncle Earl? Uncle Earl!
EARL. Joe Arthur?
JOE. All but one precinct in.
EARL. And?
JOE. You got 38,693. He's got 34,235.
EARL. Well...we won another one... You know they say the Bible says just as long as life holds out to burn the vilest sinner can still return. And, another thing, the truth will finally prevail... *(He draws a shuddering breath*

Act II UNCLE EARL 91

and is silent. Then:) And, I think this…that even though you don't win every battle, I think the main thing is—what do they say? When that great score comes to write against your name, it's not gonna write whether you won or lost, but how you played the game… And I think that has a lot to do with it… *(EARL seems to doze. JOE tiptoes out.)* I'm going to Washington…I'm going to invite all my friends up to pass a good time… *(There is a clap of THUNDER. The lights dim.)* I got so much to do…

(A slow tempo version of "Every Man a King" is played on a xylophone. EARL's light fades. Lights rise on JOE.)

JOE. He woke up and drank some coffee and then he went back to sleep. There was this coughing. They sounded like gasps. It was a funny racket. I saw he was in sort of a strain. I went outside and called the nurse. She went and looked at him and said, "He's going." And, then, he died. He just died.

(In another pool of light we see BLANCHE.)

BLANCHE. He knew… He certainly knew…what it would cost him… Politics was his life. He did what he wanted to do most. He wanted to win this election more than any other one. He was happy…

(Lights fade to rise on the Farm Area. "In the Garden" is heard. AUNTIE ALICE enters with wash. LITTLE EARL calls from offstage:)

LITTLE EARL. Auntie Alice. Auntie Alice! *(Enters.)*
ALICE. What you want, Little Earl?
LITTLE EARL. I want to give you a kiss.
ALICE. Oh, Lordy, honey. Oh, Lordy. Come on home, honey. Come on home…

(She rocks him in her arms as the lights fade and the MUSIC SWELLS.)

THE PLAY IS OVER

NOTE

This is a work of fiction. It is based on the historical record, which is rich in its recording of the actual words spoken by the participants. I have made liberal use of them—compressing and rearranging as the exigencies of the script seemed to demand. Some scenes are totally invented, but all have some basis in fact, or, at least, are suggested by the facts.

The dramatist has freedoms unavailable to the historian—the freedom to synthesize, to move in time and place, to "symbolize" rather than merely report. I have made use of these.

Given that dramatic license was taken, I do not use family names in the play except to refer to historical persons not depicted. In some cases, I have substituted a nickname or my variant on a nickname. Though these persons may be easily recognized, I thought I should extend them the courtesy of a degree of anonymity.

The play represents the musings of a dramatist on the historical record. In the course of writing it, I traveled to Baton Rouge and Winnfield (where Earl is buried in a kind of park); spoke with a number of people who remember the period; and consulted a number of texts (for which a bibliography is provided). My own memory of the times and the people was also a source. I had, in fact, a small contact with Uncle Earl myself. It, too, is in the play.

BIBLIOGRAPHY

Kurtz, Michael L. and Peoples, Morgan D. *Earl K. Long: The Saga of Uncle Earl and Louisiana Politics*. Baton Rouge and London: Louisiana State University Press, 1990.

Leibling, A.J. *The Earl of Louisiana*. New York: Simon and Schuster, 1961.

Litton, G. Dupre. *The Wizard of Winnfield*. New York: Carleton Press, 1982.

McCaughan, Richard E. *Socks on a Rooster: Louisiana's Earl K. Long*. Baton Rouge: Claitor's Book Store, 1967.

Martin, Thomas. *Dynasty: The Longs of Louisiana*. New York: G.P. Putnam's Sons, 1960.

Opotowsky, Stan. *The Longs of Louisiana*. New York: E.P. Dutton & Co., Inc., 1960.

Starr, Blaze and Perry, Huey. *Blaze Starr: My Life as Told to Huey Perry*. New York: Praeger Publishers, 1974.

Williams, T. Harry. *Huey Long*. New York: Alfred A. Knopf, 1969.

DIRECTOR'S NOTES

DIRECTOR'S NOTES